Exploring the Belief

in the

Real Presence

2nd Edition

David J. Keys

En Route Books and Media, LLC

Saint Louis, MO

En Route Books and Media, LLC

5705 Rhodes Avenue

St. Louis, MO 63109

Contact us at

contactus@enroutebooksandmedia.com

Cover credit: Marco Varrone / Sebastian Mahfood

Copyright Second Edition © 2021 David J. Keys

ISBN-13: 978-1-956715-18-7

Library of Congress Control Number: 2021953198

All rights reserved. No part of this book may be reproduced, stored in a retrieval system, or transmitted in any form, or by any means, electronic, mechanical, photocopying, or otherwise, without the prior written permission of the author.

For my wife Vickie, my seven children
(Sean, Zachary, David, Scott, Matthew, Lindsey, and Andrew),
and all those who assisted me along my journey of faith

Table of Contents

.

Introduction

"This is my body ... This is my blood ... Do this in memory of me." Simple words. Miraculous words. Misunderstood words. These words have become a source of division between Christians, the adopted sons and daughters of God. When considering the doctrine of the Eucharist as defined by the various modern-day Christian churches, one is immediately struck by the wide variety of current beliefs as to what the Eucharist is and is not and its importance. As a result, the doctrine of the Eucharist has become perhaps the most controversial of all Christian doctrines. Were it not so!

For the first 1,500 years of Christianity, all Christian sects believed that the Eucharist was truly the body, blood, soul, and divinity of Jesus Christ, what we now call the "Real Presence." What was once a sign of Christian unity, soon after the Protestant Reformation, became a source of disunity. The Catholic Church, on one hand, considers the Eucharist to be the source and summit of its faith, while other Christian groups, such as the Salvation Army or Quakers, give the Eucharist little or no role in their faith. Catholics, the Orthodox, Lutherans, some Anglicans, and a sprinkling of other smaller churches believe that a miracle happens each and every time they celebrate their liturgy, as they believe Jesus becomes truly physically present—body, blood, soul, and divinity—in the Eucharist in what previously was simply bread and wine. In fact, Catholics routinely celebrate the Eucharist multiple times daily at their various liturgy services, termed Masses. Those who believe in the Real Presence are not a small group of people. Those holding this belief represent more than two-thirds of the world's 2.5 billion Christians—that is, more than 1.7 billion Christians[1]. In between these groups there are churches with in-between views (imagine that!). The Eucharist, for them, could be a spiritual presence that becomes real when received, a strictly spiritual reception, or perhaps is just a reminder of Jesus and what He has done for us. Their reception of the Eucharist may range from weekly to monthly to not all.

On an individual basis, the reasons for one's beliefs or lack of beliefs may simply be historical—"What religion did my parents raise me in?"; "Which group did I join when I first became Christian?"; or perhaps, "Whom did I marry?"

Even those who do believe—willfully believe—may find themselves having doubts at times, or even all the time. Many simply do not know the basis for their own or other churches' belief or nonbelief in the Real Presence. Yet in spite of these concerns as to the presence or nonpresence of Jesus in the Eucharist, in my visiting of various churches, all who receive the Eucharist (in good faith) seem to be drawn closer to God. When receiving the Eucharist with due respect, they seem to be enriched by it. So, I have to believe something definitely happens there.

As I love the Eucharist, I wish others to love it, too. So, I have

---

[1] http://en.wikipedia.org/wiki/List_of_Christian_denominations_by_number_of_members (as of April 24, 2014).

written this book for those who wish to understand the Real Presence in the Eucharist for the first time and for those who wish to extend their belief to a deeper level. It is a story that needs to be told, based not only on the scriptures—as found in Old Testament typology and prophecy and in the many New Testament references—but also is a story that needs to ask other questions to confirm and validate one's understanding of the scriptures. To be complete, one should ask questions such as "What did the Apostolic Fathers (those teachers trained/taught directly by the apostles or, at most, a second generation) and the subsequent Early Church Fathers (prominent teachers and doctors of the church through about the ninth century) believe?"—for they were closest to Christ and the apostles. Remember that many doctrines, such as the Trinity and the dual nature of Jesus, were not formalized in the earliest days. It took years for the church to fully understand these teachings. Likewise, it is true that the doctrine on the Eucharist also took years to formally develop. One must ask, "How did the Eucharistic doctrine formally develop under the guidance of the Holy Spirit?" Other questions that need to be asked include "Did time change or distort those doctrines, or has the doctrine been rock solid?" and "Has God given us any verifiable miraculous interventions to help us understand and confirm the teachings on the Eucharist?"

As you may well guess, my lens is Catholicism, so you may or may not see things differently. But realistically, it is written this way because the Catholic Church was there from the beginning and has the most to say about the subject. And anyway, would you really want to read about the Real Presence from one who does not believe it?

Personally, I can say that after being raised Catholic, I simply believed in the Real Presence out of a childlike faith. Then, one day, an evangelical minister asked me to explain why I believed in the Real Presence. That question eventually led me onto an eleven-year journey in which, while working full-time as a PhD physicist in a hospital setting and also raising seven kids, I managed to obtain a master's degree in theology and came to understand more fully the reasons for my belief in the Real Presence. This I wish to pass on to others as straightforwardly as I can, raising and answering objections along the way. In the end, I desire and hope that you also will gain a new perspective on your own understanding of the Eucharist, while coming to a greater understanding of the beliefs of your Christian brothers and sisters. For me, this book will be a success if it results in a deepening of your love for Jesus Christ. What could be a greater goal? So, shall we begin?

Chapter 1

How Can This Be?

Realizing Not Everything Needs to Be Rational
to Our Senses and Our Experience

At the Last Supper, the night before He died, Jesus of Nazareth gathered with His twelve apostles for a Passover meal. During that meal, He deviated from the normal Passover ritual, took bread, blessed it, broke it, and said, "This is my body" (Mark 14:23).[2] Similarly, He took wine, blessed it, and said, "This is my blood." Christians now call this ritual the Eucharist. For some, it is merely a memorial of Jesus and the Last Supper. For others, it is a source of God's life. For Lutherans, high Anglicans, Catholics, and Orthodox, it is truly Jesus. It is, according to the Catechism of the Catholic Church, the source and summit of the Christian life, the source and summit of our ecclesial life.[3] Such Christians give the Eucharist many

---

[2] Unless otherwise noted, scripture quotations are taken from the Revised Standard Version of the Bible, published by the National Council of Churches of Christ. It can be found online at www.biblegateway.com/versions/Revised-Standard-Version-Catholic-Edition-RSVCE-Bible/#books.

[3] *Catechism of the Catholic Church*, 1324 (New York: Doubleday, 1995), 368. Future catechism quotations will be identified simply as CCC

names—Holy Communion, the bread from heaven, the most precious blood, the food of angels, the body and blood of our Lord Jesus Christ, viaticum, the medicine of immortality, the most holy mystery, and the list goes on. It is, they say, the Real Presence of our Lord Jesus Christ, confected through the words of consecration by the ordained priest, from bread and wine to His body, blood, soul, and divinity. They say this presence is above and beyond Jesus's presence in the Word, when two or more are gathered in His name or when they simply pray to Him. His presence is both spiritual and physical, human and divine—the same as when He appeared in the upper room on the day of His resurrection. They surround this Eucharist in liturgy. This liturgy also has many names—the Holy Sacrifice of the Mass, the divine liturgy, the Lord's Supper, the most holy sacrament of the altar, the breaking of the bread, the Eucharistic celebration, and many other names, I am sure.

Yet is there a problem here? The sacred host they receive looks like bread, tastes like bread, and smells like bread. The precious blood they receive looks like wine, tastes like wine, and smells like wine. Are they fooling themselves? Are they being irrational?

For Catholics particularly, this is not a miraculous one-time event; rather, it happens thousands and thousands of times, in thousands and thousands of places, *each and every day*. If this were a one-time event, we could say that such people were fooled or maybe that it was mass hysteria, that Catholics and others are just an uneducated, superstitious people or some other such sentiment.

_____

xxxx, where xxxx is the quotation number.

But this is not the case. The Catholic Church (from which came the other Christian churches) has proclaimed this doctrine for two thousand years. Far from being a superstitious institution, the Catholic Church, through its members, helped found the university system, was involved in the discovery of the scientific method, helped create international law, spurred the development of the arts, and has had many other cultural influences.[4] The Catholic Church is, in fact, a highly educated, systematized organization that shepherds over 1.2 billion members. Some of its past members were certainly highly educated and have included Gregor Mendel,[5] an Augustinian friar who is considered the father of modern genetics; Nicholas Copernicus,[6] a lay canon of the church and the father of modern astronomy, who gave us the description of our planetary motion in the solar system; and Father Georges-Henri Lemaitre, the father of the big bang theory of the origin of the universe; among many, many others. This is just the tip of the iceberg with regard to the brilliance of some of the church's members. In fact, in the United States to be a Catholic Church priest, one typically has to have four years of undergraduate philosophy, followed by four or even more years of postgraduate theology study.[7] Other countries also have similar

---

[4] For a good read and to discover how Christianity has influenced the world, see Thomas Woods Jr., *How the Catholic Church Built Western Civilization* (Washington, DC: Regnery Publishing, 2005).

[5] http://en.wikipedia.org/wiki/Gregor_mendel.

[6] http://en.wikipedia.org/wiki/Nicolaus_Copernicus.

[7] http://en.wikipedia.org/wiki/Priesthood_(Catholic_Church)#Education.

requirements. Jesuits, an order of priests dedicated to helping promote social justice and education, require eight to fourteen years of formation and education[8] and are not ordained for a couple of years after that. Most of the Catholic Church priests have a master's degree in divinity or theology, or a PhD degree, or even multiple degrees. It would appear that the Catholic Church—and similarly, the Orthodox, Lutheran, Anglican, and other churches that believe in the Real Presence—are among the most educated organization in the history of the world. But why haven't any of these brilliant individuals seen that this belief in the Real Presence is irrational nonsense and subsequently gone on to correct their church's position?

So, what gives? Are Catholics and other believers in the Real Presence all knuckleheads or lunatics? Wouldn't it be so much simpler to just call the Eucharist a symbol of Christ? Isn't it just foolish thinking to think that God would transform a piece of bread to become God? I mean, to our rationalistic minds, isn't it obvious? Isn't the thought of the host being the body and blood of Jesus simply irrational? On the other hand, isn't it just as irrational to believe that such a large group of educated people would hold on to such an irrational idea over a long period? Hundreds of thousands of articles and books must have been written on the topic by now. This knowledge that others have gained and proclaimed widely for such a long time cannot be arbitrarily dismissed just because, perhaps, it doesn't make sense to us. Rather, it needs to be examined, evaluated, and investigated for

---

[8] http://en.wikipedia.org/wiki/Jesuit_formation.

consistencies and inconsistencies. We must examine what the Catholic Church and other churches have taught about the Real Presence and why. We must be open to any truth found there; otherwise, we would fall into the trap of intellectual arrogance and perhaps end up discovering what Paul meant when he wrote to the Corinthians, saying, "but God chose what is foolish in the world to shame the wise, God chose what is weak in the world to shame the strong" (1 Corinthians 1:27).

Getting the Monkey Off Our Backs

Obviously, if we believe only that which is rational to our senses and to our experience is true, then it will be impossible to ever understand the reality of the Real Presence. However, we must come to realize that our senses and experience can indeed truly fool us at times, and that the real question then is not whether it is apparently irrational to us but whether it is true. Only, then can we become open to understanding the real reality of the topic in question. So the question that needs to be answered is, how do we come to know the truth? What is right? What should be believed? For thirty-eight years I worked as a physicist, making measurements in a hospital setting. When I and others made measurements, we never really knew the exact result; we could determine the measurement only to within plus or minus a certain percent. However, we knew the results were close enough so that we could treat patients effectively. When working in scientific ventures, there was no absolute knowledge. We believed our readings because we trusted our equipment, at least to within that certain percent. We would send our equipment away to be calibrated and confirm that nothing had changed when it came back, yet we had no proof that the measurements were absolutely correct. We would trust the answers the equipment gave us, but we could never give the absolute answer. There always remains some wiggle room. Eventually, you have to decide when there is enough evidence to know something to be true within limits, and within limits is all you can do.

In seeking truth, we must remember, in the end, that all the knowledge we acquire is based on trust and personal experience. This really is an important concept. For instance, in school we learn about history. Why do we believe what we are taught? Why should I believe that Christopher Columbus sailed the ocean blue in 1492, thereby discovering (or rediscovering) America? We weren't there when Christopher stepped off the boat, yet we trust the history books and the teacher who taught us.

Let me give you a personal example: A few years ago, my wife and I went to Melbourne, Australia. We flew from Los Angeles, and after a sixteen-hour flight, we landed at the Melbourne airport. But how did I know it was Melbourne? We slept most of the way, and even if we hadn't, flying over water doesn't exactly give you landmarks to go by. When I got there, I soon discovered that the people spoke a funny version of English and that they drove on the wrong side of the road. I thought we were in England! But soon I discovered that the names on the street signs matched the street names on my maps, which I had printed out ahead of time. We soon found ourselves at our lodging, and not wanting to profess that a major conspiracy designed to fool me was in the works (remember those who believed landing on the moon was a hoax?), I took the leap of faith and said that we really were in Australia. I had found a *preponderance of evidence* that I could trust, which was far greater than the evidence of some great hoax. This allowed me to accept as a fact the knowledge that I was in Australia. But what if I hadn't? If I still had maintained that we weren't in Australia, someone could rightfully have said that I had lost my mind. The point I am making is, information I acquired by people, books, and the Internet led me to the knowledge that I really was in Australia. I trusted in my sources. I came to that knowledge.

So we can't know truth absolutely. We need sources that we can trust. But with the Real Presence in the Eucharist, we are talking about a concept that some feel is perhaps absurd to begin with. We admit that the Real Presence in the Eucharist is irrational, according to our experience and our senses, yet we say it is true. But would this be the only thing in our experience that is irrational yet still true? Are there other truths that we commonly believe that also are not truly rational? Is rationality really a requirement for truth? Here are a few examples where apparently rationality and truth do not truly coexist: Love, we know, is real, but is it rational? We can sense sexual feelings between couples, but that may have nothing to do with love. Poets have been writing about love for years, trying to express its essence, but there is no complete, definitive answer. We can try to play matchmaker and pick people out of the crowd, but can we guarantee they will love each other? No, of course not. Love cannot be dissected in a scientific manner, nor can it be completely explained. People fall in love with others sometimes just "because."

The concept of beauty also shows no connection between rationality and truth. We have all seen objects that we consider beautiful, yet another person may just yawn at the same sight, not seeing any beauty at all. There is no rational test that will guarantee that something or someone exhibits beauty. Similarly, justice and injustice are also real but not truly rational in the sense that we can't see, hear, feel, or touch. Yet who has not been in a circumstance where they "felt" injustice? What is just in some cases seems unjust in others. However, some things are always unjust and absolute, such as the raping of a three-year-old. Who could defend that? So once again, the question in all cases is "Is it true?" not "Is it rational?"

So far, I have talked about the irrationality of realities such as love, but love is not physical like the Eucharist. Perhaps the idea that the Eucharistic host is real flesh would be easier to swallow (pun intended) if there were other areas of knowledge—rational areas of knowledge—where people believe that irrational things are true, just because they are. Fortunately, we can call on science to help us out.

Physics to the Rescue

Certain concepts in physics really are beyond rational comprehension. Even simple, classical concepts are not what they appear. We think that a tabletop is solid, but it is not solid, as our classical minds think. It is really a big void, as 99.9 percent of the tabletop is empty space, with atoms positioned here and there. When we consider that the protons and neutrons are actually composed of subatomic particles, some of which have no radius, we see how really big that void is. The only reason the lamp on the table doesn't fall through the table is because of electric fields generated by the charged particles within both the lamp and the table. We must always remember that, unlike chemists' models of molecules, there are no wooden sticks that attach to atoms that would prevent other molecules from passing through. Instead, we have an invisible, mass-less thing we call an electric field, which extends out to infinity and which keeps other molecules out. Doesn't sound rational when we think about it, because the table looks solid to us. I guess solid really means holey—filled with holes, not that other kind of holy. Our senses are fooled, yet we believe all this because it is true, not because it is rational.

What about another area of physics, relativity? Remember Albert Einstein, the man with the bad hairdo? He (and others) told us that time, distance, and mass are not fixed, constant quantities. For instance, if we travel very fast—say at 87 percent of the speed of light, time would go by very slowly, about half as fast. Consider my version of what is called the "twin paradox"[9]—a set of twins (who, by the way, also jointly own a pet dog) choose two different career paths. One twin chooses to be an astronaut and at the age of twenty is sent into space, travelling at 87 percent of the speed of light. The other twin remains home to take care of the dog. Both wear a watch that has a calendar function showing month, days, and years, while also having a super-duper battery that lasts a lifetime. In forty earth years, the spaceship returns. The twin who stayed on earth now has gray hair and is, according to his watch's time, sixty years old, and of course, the dog has long since passed away. When the astronaut

---

[9] http://en.wikipedia.org/wiki/Twin_paradox.

twin gets off the ship, his hair color hasn't changed, and his watch tells him that he is only forty years old. In the real world, the astronaut would throw his watch away and spend the rest of his life doing commercials for beauty products, implying that the beauty products help him to stay so young. But we know better. Biologically, he really is twenty years younger than his twin brother. According to physicists, then, time is not necessarily consistent from one interval to another, flowing like a river, as the song says. Time can be variable in duration, depending on the frame of reference and other features of the universe, such as gravity, which apparently can warp time. Does this sound reasonable? Isaac Newton would have thought Albert Einstein was crazy.

What if I also told you that the astronaut twin's mass would double during his flight, while his body thickness would shrink in half in the direction he was traveling, returning to normal when the ship slowed down? One can only say that this sounds most irrational. However, I believe it to be true, because experiments have shown that mass, distance, and time are not what we think. This implies that I also trust that physicists have told the truth about their experiments. Well, you might say, while the concepts are really not rational to the average Joe and Jolene on the street, the experiments should be repeatable. Therefore, you trust them. Apparently, irrationality based on the past personal experience of billions of people is not a big concern when it comes to time and space! After all, everyone's personal daily experience tells us that time is the same for everyone. In fact, according to Einstein, our understanding of reality, simply put, is that "Reality is merely an illusion, albeit a very persistent one." [10]

What about another area of physics you may have heard of—quantum theory? Quantum physics is that part of physics that discusses the reality of light and of tiny, tiny particles that make up our larger world and how they all interact. As a starting point, let's just note that quantum physics covers the interactions that enable transistors to work, which then were used in making the computer I am using to write this book. (I am so glad quantum theory works so I didn't have to type or handwrite this book.) Apparently, quantum theory is a true enough theory of reality to make things.

So, let's discuss some parts of quantum theory. As you remember from above, in relativistic physics, we found that rational concepts of time, distance, and mass did not obey the rational concepts in everyday Newtonian physics. In quantum physics, we find even more bizarre behavior. For instance, in quantum physics, the very nature of certain objects can change. For example, light can seem to act as both a wave when a beam of visible light reflects off a mirror, or as a particle when an X-ray (a light beam of higher energy) is absorbed or scattered, as in a medical exam in a radiology department. Thus, light exhibits a dual nature depending on circumstances. Not only does light show a dual nature, but particles, such as electrons, also show the same dual nature, being both a wave and a particle. The electron seems to "choose" to be a wave or a particle, depending on the situation and the way it is observed. Not only that, but in addition, electrons can move from here to there without traversing the distance in

---

[10] http://rescomp.stanford.edu/~cheshire/EinsteinQuotes.html.

between. How bizarre.

In another oddity, energy and motion are not continuous, as we normally expect. For instance, according to Newtonian physics—the physics that describes motion in everyday life, such as at what angle you shoot a cannonball so that it will go the maximum distance—when you are bicycling, you normally start by gradually building up speed and moving forward in a continuous, smooth manner. Not so in quantum physics. Only certain energy levels are allowed, and movement occurs in discrete steps. As a result, it is somewhat like living as if you are in a series of movie frames. In an old-time movie, the motion seemed somewhat jerky. However, if you have enough movie frames, and the frame speed is high enough, you would have the appearance of moving smoothly. Yet the movement produced on the screen in reality is just a series of discontinuous steps, and we are fooled at the cinema. If quantum physics is true—and indeed, our lives are not truly continuous but rather a series of almost infinitely small, herky-jerky movements—we have to acknowledge that Newtonian physics has obscured our view of the real reality of life and that we are always fooled by our senses. Our senses are fooled as to the real reality, just as believers in the Real Presence say of the Eucharist.

Enough examples? Many more examples could be given. So what's the point? The point is that science—great tool that it is—cannot explain everything. There are basic mysteries and irrationalities to the mind of man, which science just accepts and then goes about using those principles to understand the physical world. Dr. Richard Feynman, one of the most noted twentieth-century physicists, said it best in discussing quantum theory: "I think I can safely say that nobody understands quantum mechanics." And again in a separate document: "The theory of quantum electrodynamics describes Nature as absurd from the point of view of common sense. And it agrees fully with experiment. So I hope you accept Nature as She is—*absurd*" (italics mine).[11]

All these concepts are irrational to our senses and to our experience and are certainly mysterious. Why do we accept these irrationalities? Because we trust science, and we have enough evidence to believe, not because the concept itself is rational. Did you notice that I put the word absurd in italics? Go back a few pages and you will the same word, *absurd*, used in relation to the Real Presence. Keep that mind open to the possibility of truth.

We have seen that physics contains many mysteries— irrational mysteries to our senses—that are to be believed because physicists tell us they are true. Sounds a lot like theology. I am not alone in this thought. John Polkinghorne, an elementary particle physicist turned Anglican priest, has noted and written about the many similarities between quantum theory and theology.[12] Of course, we know that theology, like physics, also accepts certain mysteries as a basis for belief. Science works with its mysteries and establishes theories that help explain the physical world. Theology

---

[11] Richard Phillips Feynmann, *QED: The Strange Theory of Light and Matter* (Penguin Books Limited, 1990), 10.

[12] John Polkinghorne, *Quantum Theory and Theology, An Unexpected Kinship* (New Haven and London: Yale University Press, 2007).

works with its mysteries and establishes doctrines that help explain the spiritual world. In Christian doctrine, there are a number of mysteries, irrational in nature, that the Christian simply believes. Among these are the Trinity—three persons in one being, the Incarnation—God taking on human nature while retaining his divine nature; the Resurrection—a person raised from the dead, never to die again. Christian believers accept these and other irrational concepts without batting an eye. But as with science, the various mysteries in theology that defy complete (and perhaps sometimes even partial) understanding and that sometimes just seem irrational do not negate the truth of doctrines, anymore than the absurdity of quantum mechanics negates the theories of quantum mechanics. Science accepts its mysteries because of the evidence of their effects. Theology also has its own evidence—evidence we see in the historical evidence of prophecies fulfilled, the reality of Jesus, the occurrence of miracles in both past and present times, and the change in people's lives. In evaluating these mysteries, it is always useful to remember the advice of St. Augustine: "Seek not to understand so you may believe, but believe so you may understand."[13] At this point, I hope you are in the mind-set to consider not the irrationality of the concept of the Real Presence in the Eucharist but rather whether there is evidence of its truth.

───────────────

[13] *Ten Homilies on the First Epistle of John Tractate XXIX on John 7:14–18, §6.* A Select Library of the Nicene and Post-Nicene Fathers of the Christian Church, Volume VII by St. Augustine, chapter VII (1888), as translated by Philip Schaff.

So far, I have shown that

- science professes beliefs that are irrational to our senses;
- our senses sometimes fail to show us the truth; and
- the church's teachings—by virtue of the church's longevity, its education, and its consistency—deserve to be fully evaluated.

The purpose, then, of the rest of this book is to look at the evidence with regard to the Eucharist and the Real Presence. Is it consistent, both historically (couldn't have been true for a thousand years but now is false) and in concept? Does scripture support the concept? Was there a development of doctrine similar to the development of other doctrines held to be true, such as the Trinity or the dual nature of Christ? Is there any physical evidence that might apply (which by its nature would have to be miraculous)? Can there be a preponderance of evidence that allows us to say, "I believe in the Real Presence"?

Let's look at why the Catholic and other churches have proclaimed the Real Presence of Christ—body, blood, soul, and divinity—for two thousand years and look at it in a reasonably systematic way. We will begin with Old Testament foreshadowing of the Eucharist.

End of Chapter 1

Questions for Discussion

1) Can you name other "facts of life" which apparently make no sense, but are indeed true?

2) Have you ever experienced coincidences which later in life, no longer seem to be a coincidence, but rather part of God's plan for you?

Chapter 2

To See the Future, Look in the Past

The Eucharist in the Old Testament

O ver the course of my life, I have come to believe that to understand nearly everything to its fullest, I must understand its history. For example, to truly understand my parents, I need to see those events in their lives that shaped them, elevating them to (or perhaps deviating them from) the best persons that they could ever be. Similarly, to truly understand the Eucharist, we must first look at its prehistory. What were the events that shaped the offering of bread and wine as a sacrificial offering of thanksgiving for the Jews and for us? These events are recorded in the Christian Bible, which is a collection of seemingly different books, written in many different times, by many different authors, and even in different languages.

Prophecy and Typology

Many Old Testament events and sayings are said to be prophetic in nature, but exactly what does that mean? According to *Thayer's Greek Lexicon*, a prophecy (προφητεία) is "a discourse emanating from divine inspiration and declaring the purposes of God, whether by reproving and admonishing the wicked, or comforting the afflicted, or revealing things hidden; especially by foretelling future events."[14] For our purposes, we are concerned with the use of prophetic statements to reveal things hidden about the Eucharist. These statements, spoken or written in the Old Testament, refer to persons, places, or things that will occur in the New Testament at the time of the Messiah—or even later, at the end of time. The question becomes, "Are there any prophetic statements about the Eucharist in the Old Testament?" In the Old Testament, we find that sometimes prophecies can be very direct and straightforward. For instance, in the book of Isaiah, the fourth "servant of the Lord" oracle states directly, concerning the suffering servant, "But he was wounded for our transgressions, he was bruised for our iniquities; upon him was the chastisement that made us whole, and with his stripes we are healed" (Isaiah 53:5). The apostles interpreted this verse as directly written about Jesus. The one who is to redeem us must suffer. Because this is so straightforward, nearly everyone agrees with the interpretation that the term "stripes" refers to the scourging of Jesus. For our evaluation of whether Jesus is present in the Eucharist, wouldn't it be nice if there were an Old Testament verse that read, "And he shall change bread to be his flesh and wine to be his blood. And you shall eat his flesh and drink his blood to gain eternal life"? That would solve a lot of the argument about the Real Presence (although I am sure some would still argue).

However, while there are many instances where prophecy is

---

[14] Strongs NT 4394, defined in *Thayer's Greek Lexicon*, as presented in http://biblehub.com/greek/4394.htm.

direct, God hasn't chosen to reveal His plan as clearly in all cases. Sometimes, His message is more indirect, more hidden. In the New Testament we see the same thing. In preaching to the people, Jesus didn't always speak directly to them. Sometimes, as in the Sermon on the Mount, Jesus spoke very directly, but at other times, He often spoke in parables. The same is true of prophetic statements. So let's examine the nature of prophecy. As it turns out, there are three different common types of prophecy concerning the Messiah:

- direct prophecy—specific statements that can be directly applied
- prophecy by analogy—words or deeds in the Old Testament that typify the Messiah or actions related to the Messiah
- prophecy by similarity—Old Testament events that are similar to New Testament events

I have already given an example of Old Testament direct prophecy. This type of prophecy doesn't seem to apply directly to the Eucharist. However, the other two—prophecy by analogy and prophecy by similarity—will apply directly to the Eucharist. A non-Eucharistic example of prophecy by analogy is the story of Jonah being three days in the stomach of the whale. While there are many stories of fishing in the New Testament, none are about whales (although I guess one can say the apostles under Jesus made "a whale of a catch" on a couple of different occasions, when Jesus told Peter to throw his nets into the sea). So where is the prophecy in the story about Jonah and the whale? To see the connection, we must examine a statement made by Jesus of Himself as Son of Man. "Everything that is written of the Son of man by the prophets will be accomplished. For he will be delivered to the Gentiles, and will be mocked and shamefully treated and spit upon; they will scourge him and kill him, and *on the third day he will rise*" (Luke 18:31–33, italics mine). At this point, the connection between Jonah and the Son of Man remains unclear. Jesus, however, explains the tie-in between the two verses when He interprets the story of Jonah in reference to Himself. "For as Jonah was three days and three nights in the belly of the whale, so will the Son of man be three days and three nights in the heart of the earth" (Matthew 12:40). Before Jesus said those words, I doubt if anyone had related the story of Jonah to the Son of Man's being in the grave for three days. Again, this prophecy is not direct and requires greater insight.

As an example for the prophecy by similarity, after Jesus's ascension to heaven, Peter spoke to the other apostles concerning a replacement for the apostle Judas Iscariot, who had died after hanging himself. Peter, referencing Psalm 109:8, stated, "For it is written in the book of Psalms, 'Let his habitation become desolate, and let there be no one to live in it'; And 'His office let another take'" (Acts 1:20). This is a psalm of vindication and vengeance (as titled), which Peter uses as a prophecy about Judas. As above, this prophecy is not direct at all. It takes the insight of the Holy Spirit, through Peter, to apply to the situation of replacing Judas.

The point of all this is that while there is no direct prophecy concerning the Eucharist, not all forms are direct, and there may be indirect forms of prophecy that do relate to the Eucharist. Like many of the prophecies about Jesus, such as rising on the third day, we need to work a little harder and will have to look for inferences and hidden meanings in the scripture. Fortunately, we will not be breaking any new ground here, for scripture itself points to the use of typology to interpret scripture. So what is typology? Scholars have found "types" in the Old Testament, the true meaning of which is revealed in what are called "anti-types" in the New Testament. (In this case, the use of the prefix "anti" does not mean against but rather "something that corresponds to or is foreshadowed."[15]) A type can be a person, place, or thing in the Old Testament, which is a shadowy figure of a New Testament person, place, or thing. In discussing Old Testament typology, it's almost impossible not to include St. Augustine's statement about scripture—"The New Testament is hidden in the Old; the Old Testament is revealed in the New."[16] When the Old Testament type is fulfilled in the New Testament, we find that the New Testament "anti-type" *is always much more glorious than the Old Testament type.* This is emphasized because it is a critical concept—the New is more glorious than the Old. Admittedly, this is not a law written in stone but rather an observation of many scholars over the years. As I see no reason for the Eucharist to be any different from other typology, I accept this as a reasonable premise.

Is typology just an intellectualism? Or perhaps it's a literary device, similar to that of an author who writes a novel, slipping

---

[15] http://www.merriam-webster.com/dictionary/antitype.

[16] Cf. St. Augustine, *Quaest. in Hept.* 2, 73; cf. *DV* 16.

into the early chapters things that will be revealed later in the book when the mystery is solved. No, typology comes from history and reflects things that really happened in history. It comes from words, written into scripture over a long period, with God as the primary author and with the human author writing the words in his own fashion. These words, written long ago, suddenly relate to someone later in history. Since the words were written hundreds or thousands of years ahead of the New Testament event, there is no way the type could just be a literary device. To emphasize, it is not a literary device; it is historical in nature.

There are numerous examples of types found in scripture. The following may help to understand the process:

Adam as a Type

Adam ate the fruit that brought death into the world. Jesus gives us the Eucharist, which gives us life.

Moses as a Type

Moses was born during a time in which the Hebrew infants were slain under order of the pharaoh. He grew up in Egypt, led the people out of slavery, went up the mountain, and received God's commandments—the well known Decalogue. Moses served as a prophet, leader, and priest for the people. Comparatively, Jesus was born at a time in which the innocents were killed under order of the king. He fled to Egypt, where He was raised for a time. He led people out of the slavery of sin and death via His death and resurrection, went up the mount, and gave us another set of commandments—the Beatitudes. Moses used the shed blood of animals to obtain forgiveness. Jesus shed His own blood to obtain forgiveness (Hebrews 9:22–23).

The Passover Lamb as a Type

The Passover lamb had to be sacrificed to save the Hebrews from the slavery of Egypt. The sacrifice of Jesus, the Lamb of God, saves us from the slavery of sin.

Eve as a Type (of Mary)

Eve said yes to the serpent, allowing sin to enter into the world. Mary said yes to Gabriel, allowing salvation to enter the world.

But is the study of typology just an academic adventure? Remember the Don McLean song in the 1970s, "American Pie"? ("And they were singing bye-bye Miss American Pie. Drove my Chevy to the levee, but the levee was dry"…) So much was written about the hidden meaning of his words (which Don McLean never confirmed) and academics were having a good ol' time. Is that what is going on? Are academics seeing things never intended in scripture? Is it just a bunch of theologians saying, "Hey, look at this. Neat! It fits!"? That doesn't seem to be the case, because, as I mentioned in the beginning of this section, scripture itself speaks of types in scripture. For instance, we see Paul the apostle introducing the idea of a type. Here, Paul speaks of Adam as being a type of Christ: "But death reigned from Adam to Moses, even over those who did not sin after the pattern of the trespass of Adam, who is the <u>type</u> of the one who was to come" (Romans 5:14).

Later on, Paul writes, "They are only a shadow of what is to come" (Colossians 2:17). But not only Paul spoke of types. The unknown human author of Hebrews writes, "They worship *in a copy and shadow* of the heavenly sanctuary" (Hebrews 8:5, italics mine).

So, since scripture itself speaks of the use of typology, let's review some Old Testament typing in relation to the Eucharist.

Old Testament Types Relating to the Eucharist

Melchizedek's Offering of Bread and Wine

In Genesis 12, we see the figure of Melchizedek. Melchizedek was a king and a priest; specifically, Melchizedek was king of the city-state Salem. Melchizedek offered to God the unbloody sacrifice of bread and wine. Sound familiar? Melchizedek was from the original order of priests—those who obtained their priesthood by being the firstborn or head of the household. The priesthood of Melchizedek existed long before the more familiar Levitical priesthood. In fact, some feel that the Melchizedek order originated with Adam. Before the fall, all sacrificial offerings would have been unbloody, as death had not entered the world, and so the offering of an unbloody sacrifice fits the scenario.

It is of interest to further compare the two priesthoods. The Levitical priesthood originated during the time of Moses and was initiated after the worship of the golden calf in the desert during the exodus from Egypt. At that time, Moses came down from the mountain and was aghast when he saw the idol worship and sexuality going on. Under the urging of Moses, the tribe of Levi rose up against the idol worshippers. As a result, the tribe Levi was appointed the new ministerial priesthood, replacing all other ministerial priests at the time (whose existence can be seen in Exodus 19:22). From that point, all sacrificial offerings were to be performed by the Levites and their descendants. Their priesthood was determined by lineage. Their offerings included unbloody sacrifices, such as the grain offering, but often, they offered the bloody sacrifice of animals. In contrast to the birth lineage of the Levitical priests, the Melchizedek priesthood originated from the firstborn. Its high priest was kingly. Its sacrifices were unbloody.

As part of our Christian beliefs, we declare Jesus as priest, prophet, and King. Since God had Moses replace the priests of his time with the Levitical priesthood and Jesus was not a Levite, how could Jesus be a priest? There must have remained in the background the remnants of an earlier priesthood, that of Melchizedek. We see evidence for this in King David, who, although not a Levitical priest, dressed up in a priestly linen ephod when the ark of the covenant returned to Jerusalem and then danced before it (see 2 Samuel 6:14). This ephod—a shoulder dress—was not worn for priestly functions but rather showed the wearer to be of priestly character (Exodus 28:4), much like a Catholic priest and others wear a cassock or a clerical collar today to show their priestly or ministerial character. As David was not a Levite, his priesthood also must have been of the of the order of

Melchizedek. As a son of David, Jesus's high priesthood then also arises from the earlier, loftier, kingly priesthood of Melchizedek. This priesthood was predicted for him in the psalms. "The Lord has sworn and will not change his mind, 'You are a priest for ever after the order of Melchizedek'" (Psalm 110:4). The author of Hebrews affirms his belief that Jesus is a kingly priest of the order of Melchizedek when he writes in the letter to the Hebrews, "So also Christ did not glorify himself in becoming a high priest, but was appointed by the one who said to him, 'You are my Son, today I have begotten you,' as he says also in another place, 'Thou art a priest forever, after the order of Melchizedek'" (Hebrews 5:5–6).

Let us then examine if Melchizedek is a type of Jesus and if the bread and wine is a type of the Eucharist. If Jesus, acting as high priest, were to offer the same sacrifice—that is, bread and wine—as that offered by Melchizedek, Melchizedek would be a type, for the heavenly kingship and priesthood of Jesus is certainly more glorious than that of Melchizedek. But what of the offering of bread and wine? If the bread and wine are the same, the Melchizedek bread and wine would not be a type of the Eucharist, for the New Testament reality never merely duplicates the Old Testament reality but is always more glorious. Therefore, there needs to be something about Jesus's bread and wine that surpasses that of Melchizedek's offering. If what the Catholic Church and other churches who believe in the Real Presence say is true, Jesus, by transforming the bread and the wine into His body and blood, would be presenting a much more glorious offering than that of Melchizedek, and this would fit the requirements necessary for a true type.

This prophetic action of the offering to God of the finest bread and wine by Melchizedek is fulfilled at the Last Supper and, for Catholics and others, is fulfilled in the Mass. Furthermore, interestingly enough, through the offering of bread and wine, which then became His body and blood and was offered at Calvary, Jesus united the two priesthoods of Melchizedek and that of the Levites, as the unbloody offering of Jesus's body and blood at the Last Supper is united with the bloody sacrifice of Calvary. This union continues today in the Mass, when the priest first offers the bread and wine to the Father, and then, after consecration of the bread and wine to the body and blood of Christ, offers to the Father the unbloody sacrifice of His Son as the representation of the real bloody sacrifice of Calvary. For this reason, Catholics call their Eucharistic liturgy the "Holy Sacrifice of the Mass."

In addition, not only do Catholics and others see the priesthood of Melchizedek and of the Levites as being united by this Eucharistic act, but they also see the ministerial priesthood being transformed and elevated by Christ.

The Requirement to Eat the Passover Lamb

In order for the angel of death to pass over the house of the Israelites on the original Passover night, the Israelites had to not only spread the blood of the slain lamb on the two door posts, but they also had to eat the flesh of the Passover lamb. "They shall eat the flesh that night, roasted; with unleavened bread and bitter herbs they shall eat it" (Exodus 12:8). At Calvary, we will see Christ—the Paschal Lamb's blood—spread on the two posts of the cross.

If the Passover is a type of the salvific event of Jesus's death on the cross (remembering John the Baptist called Jesus "the Lamb of God" [John 1:20]), then it would seem that as part of Jesus's paschal event, we too must eat of the true Passover lamb.

Continuation of the Passover

In addition, the Passover event wasn't just one night. The Hebrews were also required, in what has become known as the Feast of Unleavened Bread, to continue the Passover sacrifice/meal in an unbloody manner through the seventh day. This is seen in the following passage: "Seven days you shall eat unleavened bread; on the first day you shall put away leaven out of your houses, for if any one eats what is leavened, from the first day until the seventh day, that person shall be cut off from Israel" (Exodus 12:15). We know from Genesis 1 that all people are still in the seventh day of creation. Thus, by comparison, we also are to continue Christ's sacrificial meal in an unbloody manner until the last Christian has eaten of the Lamb.

The typology of the Passover events are almost overwhelming. What is more, this was not to be a one-time event, as God commanded that the Passover be celebrated forever. "And you shall observe the feast of unleavened bread, for on this very day I brought your hosts out of the land of Egypt: therefore you shall observe this day, throughout your generations, as an ordinance for ever" (Exodus 12:17).

And again, later in Jeremiah, God restates His promise that

sacrifices will occur forever: "and the Levitical priests shall never lack a man in my presence to offer burnt offerings, to burn cereal offerings, and to make sacrifices for ever" (Jeremiah 33:18).

However, there are no longer any Jewish sacrifices. Was God wrong? No, with Jesus's death and resurrection, the old covenant passed away, and a new covenant was established, and with it, its own Passover sacrifice. We see in Luke: "And he took bread, and when he had given thanks he broke it and gave it to them, saying, 'This is my body which is given for you. Do this in remembrance of me.' And likewise the cup after supper, saying, 'This cup which is poured out for you is *the new covenant* in my blood'" (Luke 22:19–20, italics mine).

That "once and for all" sacrifice is celebrated in an unbloody manner in the Mass, which is truly a sacrificial meal, and furthermore is to be done until the end of time.

Desert Meals for Dessert?

Having escaped Egypt in the famous, miraculous exodus flight, Moses and the Israelites faced new difficulties. How would they feed all these people? The people grumbled and remembered the "good old days" of Egypt, where, even though they were slaves, they did get to eat. What they didn't seem to remember was that God was on their side and had just done miracle after miracle to get them out of Egypt. Apparently, they had left their "Team God" T-shirts back in Egypt and were unaware, because it hadn't been written yet that "If God is for us, who is against us?" (Romans 8:31). In spite of this lack of faith by the Israelites and despite the fact that the Hebrews had large herds of cattle and flocks of other birds—"A mixed multitude also went up with them, and very many cattle, both flocks and herds" (Exodus 12:32)—God chose to provide to the Israelites both bread in the morning in the form of a substance called manna and flesh at evening in the form of quail. God said to Moses, "Behold, I will rain *bread from heaven* for you" (Exodus 16:4, italics mine). "At twilight you shall eat flesh, and in the morning you shall be filled with bread; then you shall know that I am the LORD your God ... In the evening quails came up and covered the camp; and in the morning dew lay round about the camp. And when the dew had gone up, there was on the face of the wilderness a fine, flake-like thing, fine as hoarfrost on the ground" (Exodus 16:12–14). And what is this fine, flake-like bread? The Hebrews called it "manna," meaning "What is it?" Hm-m-m, clever Hebrews! And the phrase "bread from heaven" is interesting. We will hear this phrase again when we discuss John 6 in chapter 3, along with the topics of bread and flesh. Psalm 78:25 also refers to the manna as "the bread of angels," which will become for Christians a reference to the Eucharist.

And what of the dessert, as this section's heading suggests? The manna, we are told, had an added sweet taste of honey. "Now the house of Israel called its name manna; it was like coriander seed, white, and the taste of it was like wafers made with honey" (Exodus 16:31). That was probably a good thing, especially if one is to eat the same meal for forty years! But there is more to say about the manna. A unique quality of the manna was that no matter whether an individual picked up a lot or a little of it, "when they measured it with an omer, he that gathered much had nothing over, and he that gathered little had no lack; each gathered according to what he could eat" (Exodus 16:18), he received exactly enough to be full. (As I am sure everyone knows, an omer is one-tenth of an ephah, which is about twenty-two liters.[17]) This charism of the manna reminds me of the Catholic Church's teaching on the Eucharist. We may have the big host, a little host, or just the smallest piece of a host (as is sometimes given to the sick and dying who cannot swallow properly), yet all receive exactly a full, complete Christ.[18]

One final comparison: the manna and flesh were provided to the Israelites until they reached the Promised Land. So it is also true for the church. God will continue to provide the Eucharist until the last Christian has received the Lord, until that last day before the last judgment. It is hard to miss the typology of the manna.

A Type of the Trinity Involving a Most Interesting Bread

While still in the desert, God began to instruct Moses concerning the development of a central place for worship, the "tabernacle." Three principle items would be placed in this tabernacle. The first would be the ark of the covenant, upon which, from above the mercy seat, "I [God] will speak with you of all that I will give you in commandment for the people of Israel" (Exodus 25:22). The second item in the tabernacle would be the golden table, upon which the Bread of the Presence would be placed. God

---

[17] http://christiananswers.net/dictionary/weights.html.

[18] CCC 1377.

commanded Moses, "And you shall set the Bread of the Presence on the table before me always" (Exodus 25:30). Gold plates were to be used to set the bread on, and cups with frankincense would also be placed on the table. In addition, there would be "pitchers and bowls for pouring libations" (Exodus 25:29); that is, wine would be served with the meal. The third item in the tabernacle would be a golden lampstand, lit with seven lamps—a menorah (Exodus 25:37).

Interesting combination of things—a place for the one whose commands we are to follow, a source of nourishment in the form of bread and wine, and flames to cast light before it. It's not hard to conceive that these are types for the Father, Son, and the Holy Spirit. Even the order in which the instruction is given follows the Trinitarian formula: "Go therefore, and make disciples of every nation, baptizing them in the name of the Father, and of the Son, and of the Holy Spirit" (Matthew 28:19). Once again, bread and wine are used to point to Jesus.

As interesting as this typological depiction of the Trinity is, it is perhaps even superseded by the respect given to the Bread of the Presence, or the Showbread, as it is sometimes called.[19]

- Every Sabbath, the Showbread was to be placed before the Lord as a sign of the everlasting *covenant* (Leviticus 24:8), much like the precious blood at the Last Supper is the sign

---

[19] Items 1 through 6 are derived from material condensed from Brant Pitre, *Jesus and the Jewish Roots of the Eucharist* (New York: Random House, 2011), 122–125, 128–131.

of the new covenant.

- Every time the golden table was taken out of the tabernacle, "over these [the bread offering, plates, cups, bowls and pitchers] they shall spread a scarlet cloth and cover all with a tahash skin" (Numbers 4:8). Doesn't this remind you of the veil used to cover a monstrance?

- The Showbread is intended for a feast. The addition of frankincense that rises to God makes it a sacrifice also. Ezekiel, in his vision of the New Israel, describes a table before the Holy of Holies. Ezekiel calls this table an altar, which is, of course, a place of sacrifice (Ezekiel 41:22). The Showbread is a sacrifice and a banquet, just like the Mass.

- On each Sabbath, the priests performed both the bloody animal sacrifices and the unbloody sacrifices (the Showbread placement and the wine libation). After the destruction of Jerusalem in AD 70, not only were the bloody sacrifices discontinued but also the unbloody Showbread sacrifice. All Old Testament sacrifices stopped at the same time.

- When the Showbread was brought into the Holy Place, the Showbread was placed on a marble table. After being offered in sacrifice, it was considered holy and was placed on the golden table. Some transition had happened that made the Showbread sacred. Likewise, Catholics use gold and other fine material to contain the Eucharist. The use of gold is appropriate, considering who is contained in the vessel.

- During the festivals of Passover, Pentecost, and Tabernacles, when many Jewish pilgrims came to Jerusalem, the temple priests would sometimes remove the golden table from the Holy Place so the pilgrims could see it. Then, remarkably, they would raise the Showbread so all could see and say, "Behold, God's love for you." This is shockingly close to a modern Catholic Eucharistic procession or a benediction.

Food for All

In 2 Kings, we see a glimpse of the future Eucharist. "A man came from Ba′al-shal′ishah, bringing the man of God bread of the first fruits, twenty loaves of barley, and fresh ears of grain in his sack. But his servant objected, 'How can I set this before a hundred men?' 'Give it to the people to eat,' Elisha insisted. 'For thus says the LORD, "They shall eat and there shall be some left over."' And when they had eaten, there was some left over, as the LORD had said" (2 Kings 4:42–44). From a small amount, God provides sustenance for all and is not fully consumed.

In the New Testament, we will see the multiplication of the loaves and fishes. But that is not the anti-type of the miracle God provided to Elisha; rather, it is a precursor to an even more glorious miracle, where God provides Himself to the world forever, as a true spiritual sustenance. And of course, spiritual does not equate to symbolic. A spirit is real. Never call the Holy Spirit just a symbol.

The Universal Sacrifice

At the time of Malachi, the Jews were lax in their faith. They even offered blind lambs for their ritual sacrifices. Malachi condemned this practice and predicted a new sacrifice. Malachi quoted the Lord in saying, "For from the rising of the sun, even to its setting, my name is great among the nations; And everywhere they bring sacrifice to my name, and a pure offering; For great is my name among the nations, says the LORD of hosts" (Malachi 1:11).

The Gentiles' worship at that time included human sacrifice and temple prostitution. Were these the sacrifice and pure offerings that Malachi was talking about? Hardly! Clearly, Malachi was speaking prophetically about a future sacrifice to be observed continuously around the world. This sacrifice—the one sacrifice of Christ on Calvary—is represented daily all around the world in the Catholic Mass, where Catholics participate in the representation of the sacrifice of Christ. As the priest says in the Eucharistic Prayer III in the Catholic Mass, "So that from the rising of the sun to its setting a pure sacrifice may be offered to your name."[20] And what is the pure offering? What is *the* offering that in the course of time has most pleased the Father? Is it not Jesus the Christ, the Paschal Lamb, the purest of all offerings?

---

[20] http://www.universalis.com/static/mass/orderofmass.htm,   3rd edition of the *Roman Missal*, English translation, 2011.

So, What Does This Mean?

We see, in the Old Testament, shadows of what is to come. We see a tie-in to Melchizedek and the sacrificial offering of bread and wine. We see the importance of Passover and the offering of the unblemished Lamb of God. We see God providing manna in the desert as sustenance to all. We see God commanding that the Bread of the Presence and the wine be offered in the light of the flaming lamps to Him in the Holy of Holies. We see God through the prophet Malachi, requiring everywhere, for all time, a pure offering to Him. Jesus, as high priest, will merge these events together, when, as part of the Passover ceremony on the night before He suffered and died, He offers, as a sacrifice to His Father, bread transformed into His body and wine transformed into His blood, as the true, pure, and perfect Paschal Lamb, as true sustenance to all "nations" and all peoples "for the good of the many." Yet to the people of the Old Testament, these foreshadowings are just what they suggest—real shadows, not understood, and perhaps not even thought about. Certainly no one could have possibly understood that the Son of God would become man and later turn bread into His flesh and wine into His blood. However, a foundation was laid, which will be revealed in the New Testament. At this point, it has been shown that bread and wine did have a special significance to the Israelites, particularly a sacrificial significance. It would not be until the arrival of the Messiah, however, that the extent of this special significance would blossom. So next, we must examine how Jesus brought this about and how His fledgling church would continue the story.

End of Chapter 2

Questions for Discussion

1) Which of the types presented in Chapter 2 is most significant for you?

2) The people of Israel's very lives were saved by the nutrition provided by the manna, yet they grumbled and were not satisfied. They failed to see the daily miracle of the manna. The Eucharist is more glorious than the manna, yet many "believers" fail to see the miracle of the Eucharist. How can you maintain a hunger for the Eucharist?

Chapter 3

What Was Jesus Trying to Say, or Did He Say It?

The Prediction of the Eucharist in the New Testament

I n the Old Testament we have seen Eucharistic typology foreshadowing but not proclaiming the coming sacramental Eucharist. In the New Testament, the foreshadowing continues as Jesus further prepares His apostles for His Eucharistic miracle. Jesus starts out with a bang. In the very first week of His public ministry, Jesus will perform His first miracle—one that involves transubstantiation; that is, the changing of one substance into another. Later, He will, in a sense, duplicate the miracle of Elisha by multiplication of the loaves and the fishes (twice in the Synoptics, once in John). Following this, at a synagogue in Capernaum, He will tell the crowd that He will give them His very flesh and blood to eat—a very mysterious promise. So we begin.

The First Miracle of Transubstantiation—the Wedding Feast of Cana

Shortly after Jesus's baptism in the Jordan River by John the Baptist, Jesus and His mother are invited to a wedding in Cana, along with His newfound disciples. Now, I don't believe that bringing the disciples to the wedding caused the wedding couple to run out of wine at the wedding, but nonetheless, they did run out of wine. Mary, sensing the possible embarrassment to the couple, simply mentions to Jesus, "They have no wine" (John 2:3). Jesus, being far more perceptive than I, knows right away that His mother wants Him to do something about it. He says to her, "What have you to do with me? My hour has not yet come" (John 2:4), or perhaps in today's language, He might have said, "Mom, I know what you want, but the time is not right for me to begin a public ministry." Jesus knows full well that performing a miracle will create quite a stir, but being a good son, Jesus fulfills His mother's wishes. Jesus orders the servants to fill the purification jars with water. The water miraculously turns into wine. The substance of water is transformed into wine—and fine wine at that. Later, in his ministry at the Last Supper, Jesus will tell His apostles that the bread they will eat and the wine they will drink has become His very body and blood, only in that case, unlike the wine at Cana, which exhibited the taste, color, and aroma of wine, the body and blood at the Last Supper will retain the "accidents" of bread and wine; that is, the outward appearances of bread and wine, even though the substance truly becomes the body and blood of our Lord Jesus Christ. The Last Supper transformation is even more glorious as a greater transformation occurs—bread and wine are transformed into the body and blood of Jesus Christ. Thus, the miracle of Cana is a type of the Eucharist.

Jesus Shocks His Followers

Three years have passed since Jesus performed His first miracle at Cana. The apostle John tells us in chapter 6 of his Gospel that Jesus and the disciples crossed the Sea of Galilee to the Sea of Tiberius. Upon arriving on the other shore, they "went up the mountain" (John 6:4). Now, mountains are naturally religious symbols and particularly were such for ancient Judaism. Mountains are a true natural revelation of God. They naturally show us how awesome and beautiful God must be. Mountains have often been a place where, in Jewish history, significant theological events take place. This will also be true in John 6. So let's continue with the story.

The crowds, after walking around the sea, arrive to listen to Jesus's teaching. In the Markan parallel version of the story, Mark describes the grass as being green, indicating it is now springtime (Mark 6:39). John, the most theological of the Gospel writers, confirms this and directly states, "The Jewish Feast of Passover was near" (John 6:4). For John, Jesus's whole ministry—beginning with John the Baptist's declaring, "Behold, the Lamb of God!" and through the Crucifixion—is a fulfillment of the true Passover. It is as if he is flashing a neon sign before our eyes, drawing our minds to remember the Passover events, which as we saw in the last chapter was a type of the Eucharist.

The Multiplication of the Loaves and the Fishes

The crowds are gathered. Jesus asks Philip, "Where can we buy enough food for them to eat?" (John 6:5). Jesus, of course, knows the answer ahead of time and is probably smiling on the inside. Philip responds by saying there is no way they can buy enough food. But for Jesus, everything is possible, and Jesus is going to prove this point—nothing is impossible for Him. As the story goes, Jesus ends up feeding five thousand men (only men were counted) from five barley loaves of bread and a few fish. (It should be noted that barley also was used by Elisha.) To feed this crowd, Jesus took the loaves and fishes, "gave thanks, and passed them around" (John 6:11)—words He will echo at the Last Supper. In Mark's version, Jesus even looks up to heaven, just as He would also do at the Last Supper. In John's account, Jesus distributes the loaves Himself, an action He will similarly do as He distributes the Eucharist to the apostles at the Last Supper. Jesus, it would seem, is a potentially endless source of sustenance for His people. Twelve baskets are left over—twelve being a symbolic number of Israel's twelve tribes and of the twelve apostles, representatives of the New Israel, the church. All are satisfied. As this account is so similar to the account of Elisha and the twenty barley loaves in 2 Kings 4:42, one has to wonder if the Jews remembered the account of Elisha at the time. Or were they, perhaps, like most of us—just too amazed by what had taken place to connect the dots? The event certainly didn't escape their attention, for we are told that Jesus perceived that the Jews might "take him by force to make him king. [So] Jesus withdrew again to the hills by himself" (John 6:15).

This scene would be duplicated again. In Mark 8, Jesus feeds the four thousand. Afterward, Mark records the following conversation:

Now the disciple had forgotten to bring any bread; and

they had only one loaf with them in the boat. And he cautioned them, saying, "Watch out—beware of the yeast of the Pharisees and the yeast of Herod." They said to one another, "It is because we have no bread." And becoming aware of it, Jesus said to them, "Why are you talking about having no bread? Do you still not perceive or understand? Are your hearts hardened? Do you have eyes, and fail to see? Do you have ears, and fail to hear? And do you not remember? When I broke the five loaves for the five thousand, how many baskets full of broken pieces did you collect?" They said to him, "Twelve." "And the seven for the four thousand, how many baskets full of broken pieces did you collect?" And they said to him, "Seven." Then he said to them, "*Do you not yet understand*?" (Mark 8:14–21, italics added)

No, they did not understand the meaning of the multiplication of the loaves and the fishes. Nor would they understand, until much later, that Jesus was not constrained by natural laws. He could, if He wished, provide whatever and to whomever He wished. Soon, this would apply to giving His very body and blood to His followers.

Jesus Walks on the Sea of Galilee

The episode in John's Gospel that follows the feeding of the five thousand is the crossing of the Sea of Galilee, with Jesus walking on water. After being alone for a while on the mountain, Jesus returns and sends the apostles back across the sea. It is soon night.

The apostles find themselves in a boat, fighting a strong wind. It is a scary situation that becomes even scarier when suddenly they see a shadowy figure approach. It is Jesus, walking on the water, approaching them. It is the real Jesus. It is His Real Presence. Even though it was not reasonable to think that the figure (called a ghostly figure in Mark) is Jesus, Jesus proves that it is His Real Presence as He approaches the boat. Why would Jesus choose to do this? Is there a connection to the Real Presence in the Eucharist? The connection might be missed until we look at the Markan parallel. Mark concludes his version of the walking-on-the-water narrative with the somewhat eclectic statement, "They had not understood the incident of the loaves" (Mark 6:52). Mark directly and intentionally ties Jesus's appearance while walking on the water—unrecognizable at first as a real human person and controlling the elements of nature—to the miraculous feeding of the people. Just as the apostles' senses had difficulty seeing that it was Jesus walking on the water, in the Eucharist their senses would fail to discover the Real Presence of Jesus Christ. Understandably, the apostles would misunderstand—I certainly would have misunderstood. Yet after Pentecost, when the apostles remembered the feeding of the people and the feeding at the Last Supper, they would understand.

Bread-of-Life Discourse

The next day, the crowd realizes that Jesus sent the apostles off in a boat but note He had not gone Himself. Nonetheless, Jesus was not to be found. Coincidentally (are there any coincidences?), a fleet of boats arrives from Tiberius, right near the place where the multiplication of the loaves and fishes occurred. The crowd decides to get on these boats, go back across the sea, and try to find Jesus. Maybe He is with His apostles. (In my life, I have found trying to find Jesus by looking for the apostles or their successors and their teaching is always a good thing to do!) The crowd crosses over the sea. They do find Jesus. Jesus chastises them, because he understands they came looking for him because He had given them real, earthly food the day before. He seems somewhat testy (in a non-sinful manner) and states, "Amen, amen, I say to you, you are looking for me not because you saw signs but because you ate the loaves and were filled. Do not work for food that perishes but for the food that endures for eternal life, which the Son of Man will give you" (John 6:26–27).

Evidently, Jesus has a gift of food far greater than bread. Jesus has told them that He gives them a greater sign—food that endures for eternal life! But the Jews tell Him that words don't mean much; they want a physical sign. They ask, "Then what sign do you do, that we may see, and believe you? What work do you perform?" (John 6:30). Unsatisfied with the miracle of the loaves and fishes just the day before, the crowd asks for a new and greater sign, such as the manna given by Moses. Moses was their hero. Could Jesus compare to Moses? How could He respond?

The Jews were seeking a physical, real sign, not some esoteric symbol. They wanted a sign that could interact with the senses. They wanted a sign that could be seen, felt, and touched— something they could tell their grandchildren about someday. As a response, Jesus explains that the manna in the desert came from

God, not Moses. Jesus says His Father will give them a far greater gift, the true bread from heaven. He promises a sign—something real and tangible that will be far greater than that of manna. Jesus is that gift. Jesus states four times "I am the bread of life." This is one of the many "I am" sayings, where Jesus expounds on His reality. Bread, we know, is a basic substance, giving needed sustenance for life. Jesus will provide true sustenance.

But the "I am" statement is not a sign. It is symbolic language. Jesus used it often as in His statements; for example: "I am the light of the world" (John 9:5); "I am the gate" (John 10:9); "I am the vine, you are the branches" (John 15:5a). With the "I am" sayings, we naturally understand the symbolism. Nothing in the sentence structure would make us want to say that Jesus is a gate. The statements follow a specific format—"I am the" metaphor, followed by an explanation of that metaphor. The verses following the metaphor explain the meaning of the metaphor and never employ a second metaphor to explain the first. With such guidance, we examine subsequent verses to fill in the meaning of the symbol. For instance, when Jesus says, "I am the vine, you are the branches," He next states, "He who abides in me, and I in him, he it is that bears much fruit, for apart from me you can do nothing" (John 15:5b). We understand we are connected to Jesus, in union with Him. We share the very life of Jesus that flows to us. This is exactly what will happen next in John 6. Jesus will give us the symbol, and then He will take the next step to define the meaning of the symbol.

Flesh to Eat

Jesus describes the sign He will give. He has already stated the metaphor—"I am the bread of life." He will now get specific and explain what the symbolic bread really is. He states, "The bread that I will give is my flesh for the life of the world" (John 6:51). This is a very tangible, real sign. This is the response to the Jews' request as to what work Jesus would perform. He states the metaphor and then explains exactly what the metaphor stands for, as is the standard for the "I am" sayings. In this case, the metaphor is Jesus as bread, and the explanation is that the bread is His flesh. This is exactly how the Jews understood Jesus. The Jews took the declaration of the bread He would give them as Jesus's flesh. Flesh was not seen as a second metaphor.

The Jews react. "The Jews disputed among themselves, saying, 'How can this man give us [His] flesh to eat?'" (John 6:52). No question; the Jews were thinking in cannibalistic terms. Does Jesus correct this as He corrected so many other misunderstandings? No. He repeats it again. "Truly, truly, I say to you, unless you eat the flesh of the Son of Man and drink his blood, you do not have life within you" (John 6:53).

Fifteen times in John, the Greek word *phago*, meaning "to eat," is used. Could it be that *phago* is sometimes used to reference a symbolic eating? When examining the use of the term in both the Old Testament and the New Testament, we find that all uses of the word *phago* are literal. There is not one instance in which the word is used in a symbolic sense—to pretend you are eating something but really are not. Jesus continues, "Truly,

truly, I say to you, unless you eat the flesh of the Son of Man and drink his blood, you do not have life within you" (John 6:53).

Again, He has repeated the command to eat His flesh and drink His blood. Next, He will repeat the command in even stronger language. "Whoever eats my flesh and drinks my blood has eternal life, and I will raise him on the last day" (John 6:54).

This is stronger language, for the Gospel writer now even changes the Greek word used. In verses 54–58, the Greek word *trogo* is used. This word is much stronger and means "to gnaw, chew, or crunch." There is a nuance here that is important. Gnawing implies a continual eating. When we eat a hot dog, the food is there and then it is gone. When we "gnaw," there is a continuing aspect. We keep receiving juices and nourishment from what is gnawed. So too with the Eucharist. We are to continue to be nourished by the graces of the Eucharist all the day long.

And again, Jesus says, "For my flesh is true food, and my blood is true drink. Whoever eats my flesh and drinks my blood remains in me and I in him. Just as the living Father sent me and I have life because of the Father, so also the one who feeds on me will have life because of me" (John 55–57).

Jesus repeats insistently, again and again, that people are to eat His flesh and drink His blood. The poor Jews do not know what to make of this. No wonder many leave, probably thinking Jesus is crazy or drunk. All of a sudden, Jesus begins to talk about bread again. "This is the bread that came down from heaven. Unlike your ancestors who ate and still died, whoever eats this bread will live forever" (John 6:58).

"This is the bread ..." Can't you see Jesus standing there,

perhaps striking His chest for emphasis as He makes this point? This symbolic bread is this real body of mine!

Jesus—the Worst Teacher Ever?

Did the Jews think that Jesus was speaking symbolically? No. They believed that Jesus meant what He said. To eat human flesh or to drink blood was a very vile thing for the Jews, and thus, they had trouble believing what they had just heard. They spoke out. "This saying is difficult; who can accept it?" (John 6:60). His disciples continued to murmur against Him. He replied, "Does this offend you?" (John 6:61). Jesus needed to say something at this point to reassure His disciples. They probably all thought that He had gone loco. Instead of being reassuring, Jesus asked them, "Then what if you were to see the Son of man ascending where he was before?" (John 6:62).

He was talking about His Father above. Did Jesus say that He was suddenly going to start rising toward the sky? How preposterous! If eating His flesh didn't shock them, this certainly would. Surely they must have thought Jesus was speaking symbolically, or that He was mad. Yet everything said seemed to indicate that Jesus meant what He said. We, post-Ascension Christians, of course, know the reality of the statement—that Jesus would ascend to where He was before. Furthermore, all Christians accept that He did. Yet it is irrational for a body to suddenly levitate up into the sky. Why, then, do so many accept that irrationality, yet feel God could never make bread into the body and blood of our Lord Jesus Christ, as Jesus said He would? Did

Jesus have the power to ascend but not to make bread into His flesh? Were there consequences to this difficult message? Yes! Because of these teachings, "many left Jesus and returned to their former way of life and no longer accompanied him" (John 6:66)— just as they do today.

Did Jesus just have a bad day? Was Jesus the worst teacher in the world on that day? If He knew that the Jews were thinking that He was going to give them His flesh to eat, why didn't He correct them? Maybe the reason is that He did intend to give them His flesh to eat! The disciples needed to believe what Jesus said, even if they did not understand how Jesus could give them His flesh. They needed to have faith in Him. They failed to have faith in Jesus, in spite of all the wonderful things they had heard Him say, in spite of all the miracles of healing that they had seen Him perform, and in spite of the miracle of the loaves and fishes in which many of them had just participated the day before. They held their own beliefs to be truer than the words of the man they had been following for some time, whose works of God they had seen and who they believed to be the Messiah, the Son of Man, and perhaps even the Son of God.

But what of those select disciples, the apostles, whom Jesus had taken into His inner group? Jesus had one more chance to correct things. Often, when speaking to the crowd, Jesus would tell parables, but He would not explain the parables to the crowd. Yet later, He would take the apostles aside and explain the meaning of the parable to them. He did this with the parable of the sower and the seed, for example, and for the leaven of the Pharisees. But now, Jesus went to the apostles and simply said, "Do you also wish to go away?" (John 6:67). He didn't retract what He had said about anything. He made no attempt to clarify or explain His statements as something other than He had said. Peter answered for the group, saying, "Lord, to whom can we go? You have the words of eternal life. We have come to believe and know that you are the Holy One of God" (John 6:68–69). Thus, unlike the many disciples who left Jesus, Peter and the apostles, though not understanding how it could be done, accepted the words of Jesus in faith—that is, all except one apostle, for Jesus was to retort, "'Did I not choose you, the twelve? Yet one of you is a devil.' He spoke of Judas the son of Simon Iscariot, for he, one of the twelve, was to betray him" (John 6:70–71). Judas Iscariot, of course, could not believe that Jesus could give His flesh and blood and ended up betraying Jesus.

So we see that Jesus had promised the Jews a sign (miracle), and as He tells them, that sign is His very flesh and blood, which they are to eat and drink. In consuming Jesus, they will, as we will see in the writings of Paul, come into union with Him, participating in the very body and blood of Jesus. This sign—His flesh and blood—will be given at a future Passover, at the Last Supper, as He promised. In this manner, He will feed the spiritual needs of His people in a much more glorious manner than God did when He sustained the physical needs of the Jews with manna in the desert.

Answering Objections about the Eucharist

Jesus would never have advocated the literal eating flesh and drinking blood, because it was against Jewish law.

- Jesus came to establish a new covenant. The old covenant ritual laws had been fulfilled and were passed away. They were no longer binding. (But don't confuse the old covenant ritual-based laws with the Ten Commandments; they are based on natural law, and Jesus indicated to the young lawyer that they were still in effect if one wanted to have eternal life, as shown in Matthew 19:16–20.)

- If it was wrong to eat the flesh and drink the blood that Jesus was talking about, then Jesus would have sinned (which is not possible), because it is wrong to encourage others to sin (much as it is wrong for an entertainer to pretend to have sex on stage to excite the crowd during a show. Something else must be going on.)

- In cannibalism, the cannibals take the life of a person. The body of that individual at one time was a temple of that person's soul. Cannibalism degrades that temple. But with the Eucharist, Jesus calls us to enter into His very life. God works sacramentally. Jesus's very body is the sacrament through which salvation is achieved. God uses that body of His Son, not to take a life, which cannibals do, but to give life to those who receive the Eucharist. We enter into the new temple each time we receive the Eucharist.

- Jesus has already shown through the miracle of the loaves and fishes that He is not constrained by limited quantities. He can, if He wishes, feed everyone. How that happened, we do not know. The Eucharist we share is the glorified body of Christ, a body that was born of Mary and that rose from the dead. This glorified body is not constrained by nature. After the resurrection, we see Jesus walking through walls, yet eating fish along the shore. His glorified body is also present in heaven. It was not left behind at the Ascension. Again, how does this happen? We don't know. How does the bread transform into flesh while fooling our senses? We don't know, but as we shall see, it is what Jesus and the church have always taught. We should not limit God because of our limited view of reality, as the disciples who left Jesus did. The Eucharist will remain a mystery until the end of time. Remember the many examples of other things in this world, things that deny rational belief and that we can't explain, yet we still believe? As with science, just because it is a mystery doesn't mean we can't believe in it, nor does it mean it isn't true.

What about John 6:63? "It is the spirit that gives life, while the flesh is of no avail. The words I have spoken to you are spirit and life." Doesn't this indicate that it is symbolic?

- Spirit does not mean symbolism. For instance, all uses of spirit in regards to the Trinity or to angels are literal. I would not want to call God or the angels (including the fallen angels) mere symbols.
- Jesus is not saying, "*My* flesh is of no avail." Instead, He uses "*the* flesh." The term "flesh" is sometimes used in scripture to indicate the concupiscence of the flesh. ("The spirit is willing, but the flesh is weak.") Our concupiscent bodies are of "no avail." It is God's grace, which is God's

life within us, which is God's spirit within Jesus's flesh, that gives avail. But let's look at this from another point of view. If Jesus's flesh truly gives no avail, what do we do with John 1:14? "The Word became flesh"—was that to no avail? The Word, after all, became flesh for us in order to save us. Flesh sounds pretty important. And what of the Crucifixion itself? Were all those wounds due to scourging, nails, thorns, a spear, and accompanying the death of the flesh all to no avail? I know of no Christian Church that would even begin to think that. The problem really is one of language, as John often switches from the flesh being good to the flesh being bad; the world being good to the world being bad, all depending on context. The context of John 6:63 has to be one of concupiscent flesh being of no avail, or all Christian beliefs collapse, and we have yet to be saved.

- The spirit certainly does give life. We certainly acknowledge that without spirit, everyone's flesh is simply a collection of various chemical compounds. It is simply skin, meat, bones, neurons, etc. It is the soul, which is spirit, that activates the flesh and gives life. So too with Christ's body and blood. It is the Spirit of Christ that gives it life. In cannibalism, one simply eats meat. In the Eucharist, we consume the body *and* soul—more correctly, the very person of Jesus; that is, body, blood, soul, and divinity—the Real Presence.

- It is true; the Word of God does give us spirit and life. It is not symbolic. And what words did Jesus speak that give spirit and life? The words that we must eat Jesus's flesh and drink His blood, or we have no life in us. Does this mean that no one has eternal life (God's grace) in them if they have never received the true Eucharist? No. Just as Jesus said, "Call no man father," or "Call no man teacher," Jesus is using a literary technique to teach a lesson. The lesson here is that Jesus is offering His very life, which is eternal life, in the Eucharist. If you don't have God's life in you, you can't enter heaven. It is as simple as that. Fortunately, those who, through no fault of their own, do not understand that it is Jesus who saved them but who seek God can receive graces through what the Church calls the "Baptism of Desire." But who wants the bare minimum? Those who receive the Eucharist receive His life in a special and powerful way. Those who do not partake of the Eucharist really are missing something. Jesus is present when we pray, when we read the words of scripture, when two or more are gathered in His name, when He walked the earth two thousand years ago, in the heavenly banquet, and yes, especially in the Eucharist. None of these "presences" are symbolic.

What Is This Daily Bread?

Christians have been saying the "Our Father" prayer for two millennia now. It is a great prayer that was taught to the apostles directly by Jesus Christ. Of special importance to our discussion is the phrase, *"Give us this day our daily bread,"* and in particular, the word "daily." The prayer itself is found in slightly different forms in two places in the Gospels: once in Luke 11:2–4 and once in Matthew 6:9–13. The original Greek uses the word *epiousios* to describe the bread that is to be given this day. The problem is that the word *epiousios* is not found in any previous Greek literature and was coined, according to Origin, by the evangelists. Apparently, the word was created to fit this situation, because before Christ, it was never needed. Some scholars believe the word means "what is necessary for existence,"[21] and bread or other such sustenance generally is necessary for routine existence. Other scholars consider *epiousios* to mean "bread for the future day." Since Jesus is "the bread of life," and we are to be in union with Him in heaven, the bread of which Jesus spoke must be that consecrated Eucharistic bread He planned to provide for us (an eschatological reference), which is now to be given in this day and age.

In translating these verses from the Greek to Latin in what is called the Vulgate edition, St. Jerome actually translates the word in two very different ways. In Luke, St. Jerome uses the Latin word *cotidianum*, which means "daily, every day"[22] to translate *epiousios. Cotidianum* then conveys the concept of a bread that is necessary for each day's existence. In addition, Pope Benedict XVI told us that the Our Father became a daily, liturgical prayer, said before meals. Maybe St. Jerome chose the word "daily" to reflect

---

[21] Benedict XVI, *Jesus of Nazareth* (New York: Doubleday, 2007), 154.

[22] http://en.wiktionary.org/wiki/cotidianus#Latin.

that aspect in his translation of Luke.

In Matthew, however, St. Jerome seems to have tried a direct translation of the components of the word epiousios. Here, St. Jerome uses the Latin word *supersubstantialem* to translate epiousios. *Epi* in Greek means "beyond, above," as in the English term epicenter. *Ousios* means "substance." Substance is the metaphysical term used to refer to the essence of a person or object. For instance, in determining the personhood of Christ, the church speaks of the homo-ousios of Jesus (*homo* meaning same, as in homogenized milk). Jesus is both man and God, not a distinct schizophrenic entity with two different personalities. The translation of "epiousios" would then be "over, above the substance," which is what "supersubstantialem" means. This fits in quite nicely with the understanding that in the Eucharist, the bread is transformed into the substance of God, which is, of course, over and above the nature of true bread. However, it is not documented why St. Jerome translated "epiousios" differently in the two Gospels. Perhaps it was due to "translator's despair," or perhaps St. Jerome was just a smart man who wanted to make sure both meanings were retained in the "Our Father."

When translating the word epiousios, some scholars avoid using a word such as "supersubstantialem," which sounds very much like "transubstantiation." Instead, they suggest that the word is actually a misspelling of another word, *epeimi*, which when used with the word for daily would be translated as "the following day."[23] Maybe so, but it sounds too much like back flips

_____

[23]   http://irrco.wordpress.com/2010/06/13/give-us-this-day-our-

to me, especially since a straightforward translation fits so well. It could be true, but even so, the phrase "the following day" would also be Eucharistic and would refer to the bread given in the future, being given "this day." Once again this would be an eschatological reference of the future union with Jesus, which is now to be given in this day and age. In any event, Benedict XVI tells us that the fathers of the church "were practically unanimous in understanding the fourth petition of the Our Father as a Eucharistic petition." Furthermore, he says, "It is impossible to expunge the Eucharistic dimension from the fourth petition of the Our Father."[24]

Last, let's look at the implication of the other "day" in the verse and its reference to the Eucharist. Consider Christ's request that this "bread" be given "this day." This fits in very well with the very Catholic tradition of having daily Mass, a tradition that, unfortunately, many other Christian religions neglect. In any regard, whichever way one looks at the epiousios bread, whether as a "cotidianum" liturgical bread or as a "supersubstantialem" bread, know that Jesus is urging us to receive his Eucharist daily. The correct choice for translation is really not either one but both.

bread/

[24] Benedict XVI, *Jesus of Nazareth* (New York: Doubleday, 2007), 154.

End of Chapter 3

Questions for Discussion

1) The Multiplication of the loaves and the fishes in John 6 is a type of the Eucharist. One detail of the miracle is that Jesus has the disciples gather up the remnants not consumed (Jn 6:12). He did not just let the people dispose of the remnants. How does that foreshadow the way we treat the Eucharistic hosts which are left unconsumed after a Mass?

2) The comments on the different translations of the Our Father in Matthew and Luke in the Vulgate show the difficulty in the translation of Scripture into any language. If the meaning of the words of Scripture depends on the translator, how can we rely on the validity of Scripture? In other words, is there an entity which has been promised to be led into all Truth who can properly interpret Scripture?

.

Chapter 4

And So It Begins

The Institution of the Eucharist

I t is crunch time. In Genesis 3:15, God said to the serpent (Satan), "I will put enmity between you and the woman, and between your offspring and hers; He will strike at your head, while you strike at his heel." Someday, the offspring of the woman will conquer Satan. Thousands of years have passed, but God has not forgotten His promise. In preparation for this moment, God has established multiple covenants—agreements—with man, which by their nature are everlasting until completed or superseded by an even greater covenant. God established major covenants, first with the man Adam, later with the family of Noah, eventually with the tribe of Abraham, and then with Moses and the emerging Hebrew nation and again with David and the kingdom of Israel. At the time of Jesus, all of these covenants are to be fulfilled.

At this point, the woman and the man alluded to in Genesis have arrived. Mary is the woman. Jesus is the offspring. Ultimately, by Jesus's life, death, and resurrection, He would conquer Satan. At the age of thirty, Jesus began His public ministry. Three years later, Jesus was in the prime of His life. He remained unblemished by sin. He had come to do the will of His Father. John the Baptist described Jesus as the "Lamb of God" (John 1:29). He performed miracles to demonstrate His power—the blind see, the deaf hear, the lame walk, lepers are cleansed, the dead rise—in fulfillment of various prophecies of Isaiah (Matthew 11:4–5). He had come to save the world. Three years of preaching, teaching, working miracles, and training disciples led Him to this point. He was the perfect "sacrificial lamb."

But before He made the ultimate sacrifice of Himself on the cross, Jesus had one last thing to do. He would take steps to help ensure that those coming along after Him would have sustenance for the journey, so that they might follow in His path. He would institute the Eucharist. This has long been hinted at through the typology of the bread and wine of Melchizedek, the Passover lamb, the manna in the desert, and sacrificial offerings in the temple. Jesus truly stated, "I have eagerly desired to eat this Passover with you before I suffer" (Luke 22:15). He waited thousands of years for this night to occur, ever since that day in the garden of Eden. John the apostle, in his Gospel, has especially prepared us for this night. From the beginning of Jesus's ministry, John the evangelist linked significant events to the Passover, starting with the declaration of John the Baptist, through the declaration of Passover being near at the miracle of the loaves and fishes (John 6:4), to the announcement that it was time for Passover just before the Greeks appeared, an appearance that would begin the Passover/Passion sequence, the hour of Jesus's glory (John 12:20–23).

Subsequently, on the night of what is now called the Last Supper, Jesus invited His chosen twelve—and only His chosen twelve—to join Him in the Passover meal. Soon, the true Passover would be fulfilled. At the original Passover, the blood of the sacrificial lamb was spread on the wooden door posts, and the flesh of the sacrificial lamb was eaten by all the members of the Hebrew household. Now, during this Passover, the blood of the true Passover lamb would be spread on the two wooden posts of Christ's cross at Calvary, and Jesus would provide the flesh of the Paschal Lamb for His believers to eat.

Jesus also fulfilled the role of the Messiah, son of David. Now He would establish His kingdom. In Matthew 4:17, Jesus prepared His disciples for this, saying, "Repent, for the kingdom of heaven is at hand." Jesus tied the Passover meal/Passion events with the arrival of His kingdom. He said to them, "For, I tell you, I shall not eat it (again) [the Passover] until there is fulfillment in the kingdom of God" (Luke 22:15–16).

The Four Cups of the Passover[25]

In the Jewish rite of the Passover meal, four cups of wine are to be drunk. The first cup (sanctification) is drunk with the blessing. We see this at the Last Supper, as recorded in Luke 22:17. "Then he took a cup, and after giving thanks he said, "Take this and divide it among yourselves" The second cup (plagues) is drunk after the basin of water is passed around, into which Jesus and Judas dipped their hands (John 13:26), while the purpose of the Seder meal is

---

[25] With due credit to the insight of Scott Hahn in his talk entitled "The Fourth Cup" (https://stpaulcenter.com/audio/audio-archive/the-fourth-cup/)

verbally explained. After eating the Passover meal, the third cup (redemption or blessing) is a cup of thanksgiving (hence, the derivation of the name Eucharist, meaning "thanksgiving"). Normally, the fourth cup (praise) follows after singing the great songs of praise, the last of which is the Great Hallel (Psalm 136),[26] but at the Last Supper, this was not the case.

During the Passover meal, after the second cup, Jesus deviated from the standard Jewish Passover rites. Jesus took the bread, raised His eyes up to heaven, and said, "Take, eat; this is my body" (Matthew 26:26). What Jesus promised in John 6 now occurred. The bread *is* His body. He does not say it is *like* His body or a *symbol* of His body, nor does it *represent* His body. It really *is* His Real Presence—body, blood, soul, and divinity. It is what He says it is. It is His substance, even though it maintains the appearance of bread. In eating the Eucharist, the apostles received the very spirit and life of Christ. This food, this sustenance, is unlike any other food. It is supersubstantial. Normally, when we eat food, it becomes part of us; in eating the Eucharist, we become part of the food, part of Christ. We become united with Christ.

Jesus then repeated the process but this time with the wine— the third cup. He stated, "This is my blood of the covenant, which is poured out for many" (Matthew 26:28). Again, Jesus is saying "This *is* my blood." He does not state it looks like, symbolizes, or represents. He promised in John 6 that He would do such a thing. Now, He has done what He said He would do. At Sinai, Moses

---

[26]   http://en.wikipedia.org/wiki/Passover_Seder#Hallel_.28songs_ of_praise.29.

used the blood of bulls to seal the Hebrews' covenant with God. Here, Jesus uses His own blood to seal the new covenant with God. The old covenant has been fulfilled. Jesus has fulfilled the prophecy of Jeremiah. "The days are surely coming, says the LORD, when I will make a new covenant with the house of Israel and the house of Judah" (Jeremiah 31:31).

Jesus continues and commands the apostles to "Do this in memory of me" (Luke 22:19). Many feel that this verse shows that the Eucharist is symbolic. After all, a memory is not a physical reality. Therefore, the Eucharistic must be symbolic. There are a number of problems with this line of thought:

- First, one has to consider what the "this" is that Jesus is talking about. The "this" is the converting of bread and wine into the body and blood of Jesus, which Jesus had just done for the apostles.
- Second, so what if "this" is done in the memory of Jesus? Whether or not the act is done in the memory of Jesus says nothing about whether or not the act is symbolic. Let me give a personal example. When I was growing up, my father would regularly make fudge using his age-old family technique. I was taught to make the fudge in just that way. Now, any time I make fudge, I make fudge in memory of my father. The fudge is obviously not symbolic. It is real. My father surely could have said, "Do this in memory of me."
- Third, there is the problem of language translation to English. The Greek word, which is translated "memory," is

the word *anamnesis*. This word can be defined as "the faithful recall God's saving deeds. This memorial aspect is not simply a passive process but one by which the Christian can actually enter into the Paschal mystery."[27] More simply, *anamnesis* can be translated as "make present." When Jews celebrate Passover, they do more than remember when God brought the Jews out of Egypt; they participate in that exodus. In effect, they bring the past to the present. In making present the miracle of the Eucharist, the priest brings the Last Supper and Calvary to the altar.

- Fourth, the Greek word associated with the English word "do" is actually used in reference to "make sacrifice" in its other uses in scripture. The sacrifice of Jesus, the Lamb of God, on the altar now becomes the offering of Jesus in an unbloody sacrifice of the Eucharist in the Mass. The command of Jesus could be translated, "Make present this sacrifice in my name."

If all this was for show, I doubt if Jesus would have so eagerly desired to share this last meal with them. If people know that they will soon die, it would be surprising if they spoke in flowery symbolic language. They want to tell those to whom they are speaking the straightforward truth, so no one misunderstands. Far too many individuals consider only the remembering part. It is the doing that is critical, and the doing is turning the bread into

---

[27] http://en.wikipedia.org/wiki/Anamnesis_(Christianity).

Jesus's body and wine into Jesus's blood. It is no wonder that while churches that consider the Eucharist to be symbolic do get some meaning out of partaking of pieces of bread and, generally, grape juice (instead of wine), those same churches do not participate in the Eucharist very often, because, after all, it is just a symbol anyway. For them, it is nothing close to reading scripture. However, those who do believe in the Real Presence believe that the intent of Jesus is to truly give of Himself, to give His very body and blood to us, so that we can sacramentally have greater union with Him. As a result, those churches participate in the Eucharist on a weekly or even daily basis.

After the institution of the Eucharist by Jesus, the Seder meal continued. As was the custom after the third cup, the apostles sang hymns, finishing with the Great Hallel (Psalm 136). Next would be the drinking of the fourth cup, but Jesus got up with the apostles and left. (Matthew 14:26 records the action without comment. "Then, after singing a hymn, they went out to the Mount of Olives.") It is as if Jesus forgot how to say the Seder, which requires four cups of wine to be imbibed before completion. At the Mount of Olives, He was arrested, taken first to the high priests and then to Pilate, the procurator of Judea. There, eventually, Jesus was crowned king when they placed a crown of thorns on His head, dressed Him in kingly robes, sat Him on the judge's bench of Pilate, and finally presented Him to the people as their king and condemned Him to die by crucifixion (John 19). Completing the typology of the Paschal Lamb, Jesus was hung on the cross at the very hour at which the lambs were being slaughtered by the priests in the temple. All the while, Jesus refused any drink, though He must have been exceedingly thirsty. At the moment of His death, Jesus accepted wine from the soldiers. With the taste of wine on His lips, Jesus said, "It is finished" (John 19:30). The fourth cup was drunk; the Passover meal was complete. The sacrifice of Jesus was part of the Passover meal. The kingdom of heaven on earth was established (although not yet perfected).

The Institution of the Eucharist: A Comparison of Wording in Scripture

The institution of the Eucharist is recorded in four different places in the New Testament (Matthew, Mark, Luke, and Paul's first letter to the Corinthians). Each writer nuanced his writing in a particular manner in order to give the greatest meaning and understanding to his readers. For example, Matthew wrote for Jews, while Luke wrote for the Romans and other Gentiles. By examining each of the descriptions of the institution, we might gain deeper understanding into the question of whether the bread and wine truly become the body and blood of Jesus or if it is only a symbolic action.

The Institution of the Eucharist—Matthew 26

> "While they were eating, Jesus took a loaf of bread, and after blessing it, he broke it, gave it to the disciples, and said, 'Take, eat; *this is my body.*' Then he took a cup, and after giving thanks he gave it to them, saying, 'Drink

from it, all of you; for *this is my blood of the covenant*, which is poured out for many for the forgiveness of sins. I tell you, I will never again drink of this fruit of the vine until that day when I drink it new with you in my Father's kingdom.'" (Matthew 26:26–29, emphasis added)

The Institution of the Eucharist—Mark 12

"While they were eating, he took a loaf of bread, and after blessing it he broke it, gave it to them, and said, 'Take; *this is my body*.' Then he took a cup, and after giving thanks he gave it to them, and all of them drank from it. He said to them, '*This is my blood of the covenant*, which is poured out for many. Truly I tell you, I will never again drink of the fruit of the vine until that day when I drink it new in the kingdom of God.'" (Mark 12:22–25, emphasis added)

The Institution of the Eucharist—Luke 22

When the hour came, he took his place at the table, and the apostles with him. He said to them, "I have eagerly desired to eat this Passover with you before I suffer; for I tell you, I will not eat it until it is fulfilled in the kingdom of God." Then he took a cup, and after giving thanks he said, "Take this and divide it among yourselves; for I tell you that from now on I will not drink of the fruit of the vine until the kingdom of God comes." Then he took a loaf of bread, and when he had given thanks, he broke it and gave it to them, saying, "*This is my body*, which is given for you. Do this in remembrance of me." And he did the same with the cup after supper, saying, "*This* cup that is poured out for you *is the new covenant in my blood*." (Luke 22:14–20, emphasis added)

The Institution of the Eucharist—1 Corinthians 11

For I received from the Lord what I also handed on to you, that the Lord Jesus on the night when he was betrayed took a loaf of bread, and when he had given thanks, he broke it and said, "*This is my body* that is for you. Do this in remembrance of me." In the same way he took the cup also, after supper, saying, "*This cup is the new covenant in my blood. Do this, as often as you drink it, in remembrance of me*." For as often as you eat this bread and drink the cup, you proclaim the Lord's death until he comes. (1 Corinthians 11:23–26, emphasis added)

In all cases, what Jesus is holding in His hands is the "this." Combined with the word "is," the meaning is clearly demonstrative, as "this" is a demonstrative pronoun. Looking at the sentence structure in all four accounts—and forgetting for the moment that the "this" is bread/body or wine/blood—one is not led to think that the "this is" terminology actually is a "this is like" terminology. In other words, nothing written leads us to believe the sentence is written in a symbolic fashion. The problem lies, of course, in our minds that prejudge the meaning of the sentences, because in the

Last Supper account, we are talking about bread becoming Jesus's body and wine becoming Jesus's blood.

Is there ancillary phraseology that would give an indication of whether the Eucharist is real versus symbolic? While the four accounts are all very specific and use the "this is" phraseology, the biblical authors do differ in the ancillary language in the rest of the account. However, none of the authors use symbolic language at all, and none of the authors added material about a time when Jesus clarified that when He said one must eat His flesh and drink His blood He was only being symbolic.

But no writer did either of these, nor did any of the Apostolic Fathers, who were directly taught by the apostles themselves. They had an opportunity to correct a realistic interpretation of the Eucharist in their writings. Certainly they nuanced other topics, such as divorce, where two of the New Testament writers (Matthew and Paul) did indicate that there was a clarification to be made concerning the issue of divorce. But the Eucharist is always stated as "This is." They must have understood that Jesus said what He wanted to convey—that what He was holding was His body and blood—and there would be no reason to clarify.

Comparison of the Mystery of the Eucharist to the Other Mysteries

In the end, is there much difference, or is there greater difficulty for God—a Spirit, all-powerful, all-knowing, in the person of the Son—to empty Himself to become a child, born of a virgin—after all, who in their secular right mind would ever believe in a virgin birth? Is that not irrational?—or for God to change bread into Jesus's flesh? In looking at the Christ child, don't we see only the "accidents" of a human being? The child is God, yet He looks just like a baby, acts like a baby, and cries like a baby. Who, without the gift of grace from God, could look at that child in the manger and say, "That's God!"? Who could have stood along the streets of Jerusalem thirty-three years later as a young Jewish man, bearing the stripes of torture and carrying a wooden plank to be used in His own Crucifixion, staggered toward what would eventually be His death and look at that man and say, "That's God!"? Yet we say Jesus is God and man. How irrational. In the redemption, don't we all agree that God used the physical—that is, the suffering and death of the physical body of Jesus—to deliver the spiritual; that is, the ransoming of mankind? It takes the eyes of faith to see the reality of the Christ child, the God man, and the Eucharist. All three are Jesus, the Son of God. Many fail to see this reality, because they have been conditioned against it.

For instance, put yourself into the mind-set of a Jew or a Muslim. Jews and Muslims believe in the same Creator as Christians do, but they refuse to believe that God could come into history as a man. They believe Christianity is nonsense and heretical, although, perhaps, the man Jesus was noteworthy. However, they look at the man Jesus and say that a man could not be God. God is all powerful. God could not die an ignominious death on a cross. God's power is not to be found in weakness. Instead, God will come in power and glory. They limit God in what God could choose to do. Because of their preconceived notions, they cannot accept God as a man and so cannot believe in Jesus as

God.

After the Resurrection

Jesus Himself shows us that the Eucharist is not just a symbol to be used once at the Last Supper and then left behind. After Jesus rises from the dead, two disciples are on the way to Emmaus. Jesus joins them, but they do not recognize Him. He explains the scriptures to them. Still, they do not recognize Him. Finally, they ask Him to join them for supper. There, during the supper, Jesus "breaks bread." This is the very same format—the explanation of scriptures followed by the "breaking of the bread"—that has been part of the Catholic Mass since the first century. These disciples were not at the Last Supper three nights earlier, as only the twelve apostles were invited, yet it is in the breaking of the bread that the disciples come to know Jesus. It is then and only then that their eyes are opened, and they recognize Jesus. So too, for many outside the Catholic faith, it is the realization of the meaning of the Eucharist—the breaking of the bread—that will lead them to the truth.

As we know, many Christians do not believe in the Real Presence. These same people, however, believe God is all powerful and can do anything (except that which is against His nature, such as sinning), including the act of God becoming man. For some, perhaps, the real reason that they don't believe that the Eucharist is Jesus is that they just don't "feel" that God *would* do this, not that He couldn't. Having the power is not the issue. After all, if God could become man through God's power, so too bread could become God through God's power. But bread is so far below the status of man, it just doesn't seem right.

This thought process is similar to what many theologians suggest as the reason for the fall of Lucifer. Many theologians believe that Lucifer had foreknowledge that, as part of God's plan, the Son of God would become man. [28] Perhaps Lucifer thought, *Man is so far below us angels. I can't possibly go along with that!* If God became man, Lucifer would have to worship God, who also was a man. His pride wouldn't allow him to do that, as human nature is far below that of the angelic nature. This was a disastrous choice for Lucifer. And as scripture says—and as Lucifer found out—pride goes before the fall (Proverbs 16:18). If God wants to give us a gift of Himself by transforming bread and wine to the body and blood of His Son, who am I to say that He would never do that?

On the other hand, through the Eucharist, God has given us a source of grace so we can live according to the Father's will. As Catholics, we believe that while we may sin, we do not have to sin. God wants us to succeed. God will not give us more than we can handle. He will give us the graces sufficient to overcome sin and do God's will. Surely one way He does this is through the graces He gives us in the sacraments, particularly through the Eucharist.

[28] William Kent, "Devil," *The Catholic Encyclopedia*, vol. 4 (New York: Robert Appleton Company, 1908). Accessed 31 July 2013, http://www.newadvent.org/cathen/04764a.htm.

End of Chapter 4

Questions for Discussion

1) Only the Apostles attended the Last Supper in which Jesus instituted the Eucharist. Jesus only told them to "Do this." He could have told those in attendance at the feeding of the five thousand (Jn 6) or at the feeding of the four thousand (Mt 15) to "Do this", but he didn't. Apparently, authority was only given to the Apostles who were the first Bishops of His Church (See Acts 1:20 "office" -> episkopen (Greek) -> Bishopric (KJV)). The term for Bishop could also have been translated Overseer. Certainly, in Church history, the Bishops have overseen their Episcopate or their Diocese. How has this particular authority—to confect the Eucharist, been passed onto our current day Bishops? How do our current day priests get their authority?

2) Many Catholics do not believe in the Real Presence. Does the host and the wine becoming the body and blood of Jesus depend on whether the person believes it happens?

Chapter 5

Follow the Leader

The Eucharist in the Time of the Apostles

Imagine you are writing an account of the Vietnam War. What would the process be? You might record memories of the events that you recall. Even so, there would be many details that you never knew or that you have since forgotten. If you were too young to remember or were not alive at the time, you would have to go to other sources, such as government documents, newspapers, movies, film clips, photographs, magazines, diaries, or memoirs. If possible, you would interview individuals who were part of the historic events. Some of the documents might be in a language foreign to you. You would need to seek out an interpreter who understands the language. The customs of the people of Vietnam are also very different from those of Western Civilization. You would need to become educated in the customs of the people of Vietnam and of America at that time. The concept is, of course, that you would try to get as close to the historic events as possible, because by doing so, you more likely would come to the truth.

Now suppose that instead of writing about the Vietnam War, you wrote about the American Civil War. Obviously, you are more limited. There are no movies or film clips available. There are some photographs that could help. You are not able to interview anyone directly involved in the war. You could, however, read accounts written during the war, even though the quantity of information is more limited. While most accounts would be written in English, the meaning and nuances of certain words or the language itself have changed, as has American society, in the century and a half or so since they were written. You want to learn more.

The American Civil War was, obviously, a very big event in American history. Much has been written about it. Included in those writings are the accounts of soldiers who served under Generals Grant, Lee, Sherman, and Jackson. Some of these soldiers recorded what was told to them concerning the strategy and events of the war. For instance, much is known about the prelude to the Battle of Gettysburg—the movements of troops during the battle, including the mistakes made, and the subsequent memorialization of the battle by Abraham Lincoln in his Gettysburg Address. These documents not only clarify the events but also the meaning of words used at that time. There are many accounts of the war from many different individuals, and there will be discrepancies between accounts. Who is to be believed?

Go back further now and write about Attila the Hun, sweeping down upon the Roman Empire. No pictures, no newspapers, and no magazines are available from that time. The only resources you have are a few written accounts at the time,[1] plus many written

---

[1] See St. Prospers of Aquitaine's *Epitoma chronicon* found in *Saint Prosper of Aquitaine, the Call of All Nations*, edited and translated by P.

accounts accumulated over the centuries. To complicate matters even more, not only are the accounts written in a foreign language, but that language either has changed with time or is no longer spoken. In either case, you now must look to other documents just to see what the words meant at the time they were written. To find the truth, you would look for common threads. If all accounts have Pope Leo I meeting privately with Attila just outside Rome, convincing Attila not to sack Rome, then you might be reasonably assured that Pope Leo I really did meet with Attila; that it is not a fictionalized account. You would look for accounts written by those closest to the event in order to obtain the best picture of what really happened.

The same is true of Christianity. We have many accounts written of the life and teachings of Christ, of the activities of the early church, and of the writings of the apostles. Twenty-seven of these documents have been collected in what is now called the New Testament. Christians consider these writings to be inspired by God. At one time, there were more than eighty early writings associated with Jesus and the early church, which were considered to be part of the New Testament scripture. However, the same problems for evaluating these documents exist as in my example of Attila the Hun. The documents are written in a language with which we are unfamiliar and that is no longer spoken (Koine Greek, for instance). There are many different manuscripts of the same documents and many different versions of each of the Gospel accounts. The manuscripts differ in choice of words,

---

De Letter, SJ (Series *Ancient Christian writers* 14), 1952.

additions and deletions of verses, and content, including which stories are told and in what order. All the documents have been edited to some degree. How are we to know the truth? To resolve this issue, in the late fourth century, the Catholic Church gathered at the Councils of Carthage and Hippo to determine which documents were truly God-inspired scripture. Questions arise: Why were most of the eighty or so documents rejected, while twenty-seven were kept? For us, centuries later, reading these documents—even assuming we have the correct documents—the question becomes "How do we correctly interpret the words of these documents?" This is not an easy task, as evidenced by the fact that there are so many Christian churches with so many different interpretations of the documents. The answer does not lie in the documents themselves. The best answer lies in answering the question "What has the church always taught from the beginning?" That is the key, for from the beginning, Jesus promised the apostles that they (and therefore, their successors) would be "guided by the Spirit of truth into all the truth" (John 16:13).

What did those directly trained by Jesus, including the apostle Paul, believe? Paul, of course, was unique and was not trained by Jesus during His earthly life; rather, he was converted and given revelation directly by Christ on the road to Damascus. The other apostles, as a group, were not prolific writers. We do have the Gospels of Matthew and John, plus letters from Peter and Jude (who may not even have been Jude the apostle but perhaps Jude the relative of Jesus), plus letters from James and John. Many other documents exist, such as the gospel of Thomas, which contain passages inconsistent with the other Christian literature and are now believed to be written by others at a much later date. The Eucharist, as portrayed in the Gospels of Matthew, Mark, Luke, and John, has already been discussed. What remains are references to the Eucharist found in the first group of the early church, as contained in the New Testament writings of Paul, the writer of Hebrews; in Luke's description of the early church, as found in the Acts of the apostles; in references to the agape meal in 2 Peter and Jude; and finally, information about the heavenly banquet contained in the Revelation of John.

Paul

To see what Paul has to say about the Eucharist, let's go to his first letter to the Corinthians. The church at Corinth was one of the earliest churches established by the apostles. They were very much caught up in the things of the world. Though they were baptized, many continued to worship idols and pursue sexual immorality, and some were even getting drunk during the worship service. To them, Paul writes:

> I am speaking as to sensible people; judge for yourselves what I am saying. The cup of blessing that we bless, is it not a participation in the blood of Christ? The bread that we break, is it not a participation in the body of Christ? Because the loaf of bread is one, we, though many, are one body, for we all partake of the one loaf. Look at Israel according to the flesh; are not those who eat the sacrifices participants in the altar? So what am I

saying? That meat sacrificed to idols is anything? Or
that an idol is anything? No, I mean that what they
sacrifice, (they sacrifice) to demons, not to God, and I
do not want you to become participants with demons.
You cannot drink the cup of the Lord and also the cup
of demons. You cannot partake of the table of the Lord
and of the table of demons. (1 Corinthians 10:15–21)

Catholic teaching has always held that from the beginning, the
Eucharist has been practiced by the church as part of its liturgy. On
the very first day after Christ rose from the dead, Christ Himself
celebrated the "breaking of the bread" on the way to Emmaus. Here
in 1 Corinthians, it is quite evident that the "breaking of the bread"
was a common occurrence. Paul is rhetorically asking the
Corinthians a question to which he already knows the answer. Paul
is teaching that when one receives the blessed bread and wine, one
is directly participating in and uniting with the body and blood of
Christ. All are one, because they all share in the same body and
blood of Jesus. If, indeed, the Eucharist is just a symbol, why does
Paul bother to talk about a participation in the body and a
participation in the blood of Jesus? It would have been easier to just
say, "It's a participation in Jesus." The words recorded in scripture
are important. Paul must have a reason for stating "participation *in
the body*" and "participation *in the blood*" (emphasis mine). (If only
Paul had thought of the idea of italicizing words, how differently
we might be reading scripture! Alas, at that time the ancient writers
were struggling even with the concept of adding spaces between
words!)

Paul surely knew the discourse that John would eventually record in what we now call John 6—that as soon as Jesus began telling the disciples that they must eat His flesh and drink His blood, so many disciples left and followed Him no more. The statements about eating His flesh and blood didn't work well for Jesus. I would think Paul would have wanted to avoid unnecessary conflict, if possible, unless, of course, what he is saying is a true and necessary part of the description of what is happening.

Note that Paul is also comparing the sacrifices to demons on pagan altars (tables), the meat of which the pagans eat, to the sacrifice of Christ, which the Corinthians partake at the table of the Lord. Although I never have been at a demonic worship, I suspect the goal of demon worshippers is to somehow participate with the demons. I do believe that participation with demons can be real and that one of Satan's greatest lies is to convince us that demons do not exist. I certainly do not consider Satan worship to be a symbolic participation in evil in the world's cultures. To participate with demons is to participate spiritually only, as demons are only spirits. To participate with Christ requires that we participate fully, bodily and spiritually, as Jesus is fully body and spirit. Hence, participating with Christ means to participate fully with His person, and that means we must partake in the Real Presence—body, blood, soul, and divinity.

Paul goes on to discuss the meetings, which are the services they routinely held. The original services often consisted of the Eucharistic service as part of an agape (love) feast, which was a meal, including wine and food other than just bread. A portion of the wine and bread would be consecrated. Because of abuses such as this in Corinth, the Eucharistic feast would later be separated from the agape meal.

Paul writes:

> In giving this instruction, I do not praise the fact that your meetings are doing more harm than good. First of all, I hear that when you meet as a church there are divisions among you, and to a degree I believe it; there have to be factions among you in order that (also) those who are approved among you may become known. When you meet in one place, then, it is not to eat the Lord's supper, for in eating, each one goes ahead with his own supper, and one goes hungry while another gets drunk. Do you not have houses in which you can eat and drink? Or do you show contempt for the church of God and make those who have nothing feel ashamed? What can I say to you? Shall I praise you? In this matter I do not praise you. (1 Corinthians 11:17–22)

Here it is again evident that the purpose of the gathering was intended to be participation in the Lord's Supper, which is the "breaking of the bread," another name for the Eucharist. Many Corinthians simply did not have the proper attitude.

As stated above, Paul received revelation directly from Jesus as part of his conversion; however, in only one instance does Paul say exactly what that revelation contained. Paul states:

> For I received from the Lord what I also handed on to you, that the Lord Jesus, on the night he was handed

> over, took bread, and, after he had given thanks, broke
> it and said, "This is my body that is for you. Do this in
> remembrance of me." In the same way also the cup,
> after supper, saying, "This cup is the new covenant in
> my blood. Do this, as often as you drink it, in
> remembrance of me." For as often as you eat this bread
> and drink the cup, you proclaim the death of the Lord
> until he comes. (1 Corinthians 11:23–26)

The language contained here is nearly identical to that contained in Matthew's, Mark's, and Luke's Gospels. Very few direct words of Jesus are given to us by Paul. Paul really wasn't too concerned with discussing the parables or miracles of Jesus. If you think about it, these words of consecration must really have been important for Jesus to personally teach them to Paul. Jesus wanted Paul to know exactly what to do and what to say. These are the words, liturgical words, to be said as part of the Eucharistic celebration, a celebration that, we shall see, was initially only to be performed by an apostle or a bishop appointed by the apostles. Later, the church ruled that bishops could appoint presbyters (the etymological source of the word for priests) to also perform this function.

Let's see if Paul believed the Eucharist was symbolic.

> Therefore whoever eats the bread or drinks the cup of
> the Lord unworthily will have to answer for the body
> and blood of the Lord. A person should examine
> himself, and so eat the bread and drink the cup. For
> anyone who eats and drinks without discerning the

body, eats and drinks judgment on himself. That is why many among you, are ill and infirm, and a considerable number are dying. If we discerned ourselves, we would not be under judgment; but since we are judged by (the) Lord, we are being disciplined so that we may not be condemned along with the world. (1 Corinthians 11:27–32)

If the Eucharist were symbolic, there would be a problem. Can a symbol result in one becoming ill? Or is it that the Corinthians were symbolically becoming ill, symbolically infirm, and symbolically dying? Context suggests that Paul really felt the cause of their maladies was their lack of discernment that the bread and wine truly were changed into Christ's body and blood. An improper attitude in the reception of the Eucharist can be judged and disciplined by the Lord. Another Catholic teaching concerning the Eucharist is given support by this passage. Catholic Church teaching always has taught that one receives the Real Presence by consuming the consecrated host *or* the consecrated wine. Here, Paul confirms that reality by speaking of eating the bread *or* drinking the cup of the Lord unworthily. This passage is also consistent with the Catholic practice that you may not receive the Eucharist unless you are in the state of grace, and you do realize that the bread and wine have become the body and blood of Christ.

Some feel that Paul is referring to the church when he speaks of discerning the body, that they are not discerning that the church is the body of Christ. Certainly the Corinthians who were getting drunk at the services did not have a strong sense that the church, of which they were members, was truly the body of Christ. But like many scripture passages, there is often more than one layer of understanding. Each of the layers must contain truth and be consistent with the others. Here, the first layer is the literal. Paul has been speaking directly about the Eucharist. It is not difficult to see that these verses could have the spiritual inference of Christ's church. The church is inferred but at a secondary level.

This also brings up another point. Many have difficulty seeing the bread and wine as becoming the body and blood of Christ and that through eating the Eucharist we become united with Christ. Yet on the other hand, Christians routinely say that the church is the body of Christ. If the union of the church with the body of Christ is also symbolic, the faith has been watered down. Continuing this way, the faith eventually becomes all symbolic. No miracle is considered real. The resurrection is just a symbolic belief.

The church, after all, is also the bride of Christ, and in a true marriage, "they become one flesh" (Genesis 2:24). With conjugal love, physically, the two are united. As Paul states, "Do you not know that whoever is united to a prostitute becomes one body with her?" (1 Corinthians 6:16). Is the church *like* a bride, or is it a bride? If the members of the church truly consume the body and blood of Jesus—or as Paul states it, the Eucharist is a "participation of the body of Christ" (1 Corinthians 10:16)—then, just as in the marital situation, "they become one flesh." It is a real participation in the body of Christ. Christ does have a body in heaven. He did not remove His body when He ascended into heaven. The body that we share is not just the pre-resurrection body; it is His glorified body—the one that passed through walls and could appear and disappear. It is truly everything that Jesus is—His body, blood, soul, and divinity.

The Writer of Hebrews

While the author of Hebrews is not identified, historically, some believe that the writer is Paul. Others believe that while the writing may have many Pauline characteristics in theology, style, and vocabulary, it is significantly different enough that they believe another early church member wrote the document. The letter is to the Hebrews, but to which Hebrews is not clear. For instance, many believe that it was written to bolster the faith of the Christian Jews in Jerusalem during a time of persecution, while others believe it was written as a homily to Christian Jews in Alexandria, during the Jewish Feast of Atonement. Regardless of its true origin, the church believes that the letter contains the truth of the gospel as taught by the apostles. As such, the letter to the Hebrews was included by the church in its canon of the New Testament. For simplicity's sake, I will call this writer Paul.

In the letter to the Hebrews, Paul refers to Jesus as the high priest—the high priest who offered Himself as a sacrifice for the remission of sins, "once and for all" (Hebrews 10:10). Catholic Church teaching states that each and every Mass is a sacrifice, yet the Catholic Church believes that Jesus's sacrifice was "once and for all." It seems like a contradiction. Looking to scripture, in Hebrews 9:23, surprisingly, we see Paul refer to sacrifice in the plural: "Therefore, it was necessary for the copies of the heavenly things to be purified by these rites, but the heavenly things themselves by better sacrifices than these." Paul could be confused, or this could be a grammatical error, which may have occurred due to the centuries of copying and recopying the scriptures. Of course, there is a better explanation. The church has long looked to the prophecy of Malachi. "For from the rising of the sun, even to its setting, my name is great among the nations; And everywhere they bring sacrifice to my name, and a pure offering; For great is my name among the nations, says the LORD of hosts" (Malachi 1:11). In this prophecy, the church believes that the Eucharistic offerings in the Mass are the "once and for all" offering of Jesus as the sacrifice of atonement. These offerings occur day and night on altars throughout the world and are the sacrifices mentioned in Malachi. This does not mean that Jesus is sacrificed again. Rather, it means that Jesus's sacrifice knows no bounds of time. In each Mass, the very sacrifice of Calvary is represented ("anamnesis"; see chapter 4) before our eyes.

Revelation

In Hebrews, we see that Jesus is a priest forever. Paul states, "He [Jesus] holds his priesthood permanently, because he continues forever" (Hebrews 7:24). Since Jesus's sacrifice is "once and for all," it would seem that there is no longer any need for Jesus to remain a priest. Yet we see that Jesus will indeed offer a sacrifice forever. As a priest, He will offer His sacrifice on the cross forever. We see this eternal sacrifice in the book of Revelation. In Revelation, which is certainly about heaven, we note the continual reference to the Passover; the Lamb is mentioned twenty-eight times—certainly a reference to the Paschal Lamb, sacrificed to atone for the sins of the world. The Passover feast evidently was a significant event. In Revelation 5:6, we see the lamb, who is slain, still standing. "Then I saw standing in the midst of the throne and the four living creatures and the elders, a Lamb that seemed to have been slain."

The one sacrifice of Christ, while occurring once in the framework of human history at Calvary, is ongoing forever in heaven in the celestial frame, which knows no time. One would say that the sacrifice of Calvary is continually made present (anamnesis) in heaven.

In addition, the book of Revelation is filled with references to the Catholic Mass (in one of its many interpretive levels). [2] Revelation contains the readings, incense, the vestments, trumpets, the "Holy, holy, holy," references to the Lamb, choirs, the heavenly banquet, etc. that are standard as part of the Mass. One could say the Catholic Mass is truly fulfilled in the heavenly mass, which is our hope to share in someday.

Acts of the Apostles

The Acts of the apostles, written by Luke, gives us another glimpse into the early church. After Jesus ascended into heaven, the fearful apostles, Mary, and other disciples remained huddled in the upper

---

[2] See Scott Hahn, *The Lamb's Supper* (New York: Doubleday, 1999), for a well-written discussion of the Mass as found in Revelation.

room, waiting for the Paraclete that Jesus had promised to send. On the day of Pentecost, the Spirit descended on the apostles in the form of tongues of fire. No longer fearless and led by Peter, they began to act out the ministry for which they had been trained. Here we see in five elements of that ministry—baptizing, bestowing the Spirit, teaching, the breaking of the bread, and the prayers:

> Peter said to them, "Repent and be baptized, every one of you, in the name of Jesus Christ for the forgiveness of your sins; and you will receive the gift of the holy Spirit. For the promise is made to you and to your children and to all those far off, whomever the Lord our God will call." He testified with many other arguments, and was exhorting them, "Save yourselves from this corrupt generation." Those who accepted his message were baptized, and about three thousand persons were added that day. They devoted themselves to the teaching of the apostles and to the communal life, to the breaking of the bread and to the prayers. (Acts 2:38–42)

The apostles didn't merely do these things; they were devoted to them. They were devoted to the breaking of the bread. They did not merely perform "the breaking of the bread" once or twice a year, as many Christian churches do nowadays, if at all. "The breaking of the bread" was an integral part of their worship.

The phrase "to the prayers" is also of interest. Remember that these were public prayers, spoken in specific households where the early Christians were gathered for the Eucharist. The Catholic

Church believes that this expression of the "breaking of the bread" and "the prayers" refers to the early Eucharistic liturgy; that is, the Mass.[3]

Luke continues, "Every day they devoted themselves to meeting together in the temple area and to breaking bread in their homes. They ate their meals with exultation and sincerity of heart, praising God and enjoying favor with all the people. And every day the Lord added to their number those who were being saved" (Acts 2:46–47).

Daily, they broke the bread. Sounds more and more like the Catholic practice of saying the Mass daily, offering sacrifices throughout the world, from the rising of the sun to its setting, as prophesied in Malachi.

Later in Acts, we see Luke, together with Paul and the early converts in Troas. What are they doing? We find Paul teaching and—what else?—breaking bread.

"On the first day of the week, when we gathered to break bread, Paul spoke to them because he was going to leave on the next day, and he kept on speaking until midnight" (Acts 20:7).

And in a mirroring of real life, we see a youth named Eutychus at this service, bored, evidently not understanding or caring about what is going on but nonetheless at the service. I guess Eutychus might have said, "I don't get much out of this service. It is bor-r-r-ring!" Here is what happens:

> There were many lamps in the upstairs room where we were gathered, and a young man named Eutychus who

---

[3] CCC 2624.

> was sitting on the window sill was sinking into a deep
> sleep as Paul talked on and on. Once overcome by sleep,
> he fell down from the third story and when he was
> picked up, he was dead. Paul went down, threw himself
> upon him, and said as he embraced him, "Don't be
> alarmed; there is life in him." Then he returned upstairs,
> broke the bread, and ate; after a long conversation that
> lasted until daybreak, he departed. (Acts 20:8–11)

Unfortunately, that is the way many youth and adults see the Mass. That's because they do not understand what is really going on. What did Paul do? Did he change the form of worship to make it more entertaining? Get a band, set a stage, have some tambourines? No, he continued with his Mass and "broke the bread" and continued his teaching until daybreak. (And we think our homilies are long!)

Later in Acts, Paul is on a boat and is besieged by a storm. What does Paul do but celebrate the breaking of the bread. "Until the day began to dawn, Paul kept urging all to take some food. He said, 'Today is the fourteenth day that you have been waiting, going hungry and eating nothing. I urge you, therefore, to take some food; it will help you survive. Not a hair of the head of anyone of you will be lost.' When he said this, he took bread, gave thanks to God in front of them all, broke it, and began to eat" (Acts 27:33–35).

Yes, the food God has provided, the Eucharist, will certainly help us to survive the storms in our lives. It is our spiritual sustenance.

Peter and Jude

In Jude and in 2 Peter, we see references to a love feast.

> Similarly, these dreamers nevertheless also defile the
> flesh, scorn lordship, and revile glorious beings. Yet the
> archangel Michael, when he argued with the devil in a
> dispute over the body of Moses, did not venture to
> pronounce a reviling judgment upon him but said,
> "May the Lord rebuke you!" But these people revile
> what they do not understand and are destroyed by what
> they know by nature like irrational animals. Woe to
> them! They followed the way of Cain, abandoned
> themselves to Balaam's error for the sake of gain, and
> perished in the rebellion of Korah. These are blemishes
> on your *love feasts*, as they carouse fearlessly and look
> after themselves. They are waterless clouds blown about
> by winds, fruitless trees in late autumn, twice dead and
> uprooted. (Jude 1:8–12, italics added)

The love feasts mentioned here are the so-called agape feasts,
which were originally incorporated as part of the service as
referenced by Paul in his letter to the Corinthians. This is further
evidence that the breaking of the bread was an integral part of the
early church service.

And again in 2 Peter 2:12–13, "But these people, like irrational
animals born by nature for capture and destruction, revile things
that they do not understand, and in their destruction they will also
be destroyed, suffering wrong [in their *love feasts*] as payment for

wrongdoing. Thinking daytime revelry a delight, they are stains and defilements as they revel in their deceits while carousing with you."

This reference to "love feasts" is not found in all manuscripts, but the storyline is the same as that in Jude and in Corinthians.

Continuing the Story

The writings contained in the New Testament distinctively paint a consistent picture of the ongoing breaking of the bread by the apostles after they had received the Spirit at Pentecost. It was a daily occurrence for the apostles and an integral part of their ministry. But in the normal course of life, we all do die, and so did the apostles. The apostles had faithfully obeyed the Lord's command to "Do this in memory of me," and the apostles had successfully established successors to take their places. But their hard work would be of no avail if those who followed them preached a different gospel. However, if their words and deeds were consistent with what the Bible records, then we have even greater faith in the words of scripture. To see if they remained true to the teaching of Jesus, we need to first examine the works of the Apostolic Fathers (those who were either taught directly by the apostles or, at most, a second generation). Then we need to examine the works of the Early Church Fathers (those prominent teachers and doctors of the church through about the ninth century). So, what did they teach? What did they do?

End of Chapter 5

Questions for Discussion

1) John's gospel is believed to have been written much later than the gospels of Matthew, Mark, and Luke. If the Eucharist is so significant, why didn't John write about the institution of the Eucharist. Instead, John seems to write about everything else that happened on that last Passover night before Jesus died. Why is that?

2) It has been said by some that the Eucharist is medicine for the spiritually sick. Paul said the opposite. He said that receiving the Eucharist unworthily makes one gravely ill. How can you reconcile these disparate concepts?

Chapter 6

A Continuing Saga

The Eucharist in the Early Church

W hen I told a close evangelical friend of mine that I was going to write on the teachings of the Apostolic Fathers and the Early Church Fathers concerning the Eucharist, he said, "Don't bother. We are Bible-based."

But if I followed that advice, I would be missing so much. The Gospels will always have a preeminence in scripture, followed by the other New Testament writings and the Old Testament writings. Those writings are inspired. They give revelation. The Bible, a source of truth, does not have sole rights to the truth. Math books can give truth—for example 2 + 2 truly equals 4—and cookbooks can tell you how to bake a cake, but neither gives revelation, nor do they claim to be inspired by God. The church, we are told in scripture, is "the pillar and bulwark of the truth" (1 Timothy 3:15), so one would think their writings, at least under certain strict conditions, must contain truth. After all, Jesus told the apostles, "the Advocate, the Holy Spirit, whom the Father will send in my name, will teach you everything, and remind you of all that I have said to you" (John 14:26). So, concerning the writings of the Apostolic Fathers and Early Church Fathers (I shall refer to both as "Early Church Fathers" in the remainder of this chapter), the question is "Are the writings reliable?" Do they contain truth? To answer this, we will look at some of their writings concerning the Eucharist and their consistency with the inspired scripture found in the Bible.

Because the Early Church Fathers lived at a time that was so close to the actual time and teachings of Christ and the apostles, the Early Church Fathers' writings are important for helping to understand the early Christian faith and in giving supplemental information. For instance, without the Early Church Fathers, we have no indication who are the primary authors of the Gospels of Matthew, Mark, and John, along with many of the epistles. Knowing the author is not critical, but it is helpful and gives greater insight. When the Councils of Hippo and Carthage met in the late fourth century in order to determine which books belonged in the canon of the scripture, they utilized the Early Church Fathers' writings to help determine which of the eighty or so documents, which were promoted by various groups, should be in the New Testament canon. Those councils didn't have the Bible to guide them. Their task was to determine what were the teachings of the apostles and what the Church always has taught. They looked, in part, to the writings of the Early Church Fathers to see what was taught in the past. Based on that information, many of the proposed documents, such as the gospel of Thomas, were eliminated due to inconsistencies with the teachings of the early church. Other books, such as the letter of Clement to the Corinthians, were eliminated simply because they were seen as second-generation documents. Other documents, such as the Didache—the teaching of the apostles, one of the earliest documents, even predating some of the Gospels—were not included, perhaps because only incomplete versions were available at the time of the Councils. In the end, only twenty-seven documents remained and were included in the New Testament. But the point is not how we got the Bible but that the Early Church Fathers' writings gave evidence and insight into the teachings of the early church. Indeed, my Bible-based friend unknowingly relied on the teachings of the Early Church Fathers as the very basis of his faith. The Early Church Fathers' writings are extremely important. If we see a common element in all such writings, then we must conclude that that element has always been part of the church's teaching. We now look at what the Early Church Fathers had to say about the Eucharist.

The Didache Teaching of the Twelve Apostles

The Didache is one of the earliest Christian documents, is known as the teaching of the twelve apostles, and dates from the first century. In sections 9 and 10, we find:[1]

> "Let no one eat or drink of this Eucharist unless he has been baptized in the name of the Lord; for concerning this the Lord also said: 'Do not give to the dogs what is holy.'"

---

[1]   William Jurgens, *The Faith of the Early Fathers*, vol. 1 (Collegeville, Minnesota: Liturgical Press, 1970), 3.

> "And on the Lord's day, gather together and break bread and give thanks, first confessing your sins so that your sacrifice might be pure."

The breaking of the bread not only was an integral part of the Sunday liturgy, but it also was declared to be holy—not bad if it is just a symbol. But we know a symbol can't be holy. Perhaps those first-century Christians were misled. Or perhaps they really believed the Eucharist was the body and blood of their Lord Jesus Christ. Now that would be holy! Note also that the Eucharist was considered a sacrifice, in line with the prophecy of Malachi.

Ignatius of Antioch

Ignatius was a bishop over Antioch who heard the Gospel preached directly from the mouth of John the apostle. One would think that his views would reflect the views of John. So if Ignatius writes something about the Eucharist, it is reasonable to presume that the writing would be consistent with the teaching of John the apostle. Ignatius is particularly noted for seven letters he wrote to various churches as he headed as a prisoner toward Rome, which resulted in his martyrdom. Let's see what he had to say about the Eucharist:

> "I have no taste for corruptible food nor for the pleasures of this life. I desire the bread of God, which is the flesh of Jesus Christ, who was of the seed of David; and for drink I desire his blood, which is love incorruptible." (Ignatius's letter to the Romans 7:3 [AD

110])²

"Take note of those who hold heterodox opinions on
the grace of Jesus Christ which has come to us, and see
how contrary their opinions are to the mind of God …
They abstain from the Eucharist and from prayer
because they do not confess that the Eucharist is the
flesh of our Savior Jesus Christ, flesh which suffered for
our sins and which that Father, in his goodness, raised
up again. They who deny the gift of God are perishing
in their disputes." (Ignatius's letter to the Smyrnaeans
6:2–7:1 [AD 110])³

We see from these passages that Ignatius truly believed that
Jesus gives us His very flesh in the Eucharist. We can also see that
there were skeptics—individuals who, like those noted by Paul in
his letter to the Corinthians, did not recognize the body of Christ
in the bread that they shared. But in all cases, the official voices of
the church condemned such unbelief. There will always be those
who do not believe.

Justin Martyr

In an effort to stop the persecution of Christians, Justin Martyr
wrote to the emperor of Rome and explained the Christian
worship service. He wrote:

---

² Cited in Jimmy Akin, *The Fathers Know Best* (El Cajon, CA:
Catholic Answers, Inc., 2010), 293.

³ Ibid.

We call this food Eucharist, and no one else is permitted to partake of it, except one who believes our teaching to be true and who has been washed in the washing which is for the remission of sins and for regeneration [i.e., has received baptism] and is thereby living as Christ enjoined. For not as common bread nor common drink do we receive these; but since Jesus Christ our Savior was made incarnate by the word of God and had both flesh and blood for our salvation, so too, as we have been taught, the food which has been made into the Eucharist by the Eucharistic prayer set down by him, and by the change of which our blood and flesh is nurtured, is both the flesh and the blood of that incarnated Jesus. (First Apology 66 [AD 151])[4]

Simply put, this is the description of the Eucharistic part of the early Christian worship service of the church, which by this time was already calling itself Catholic. This is the identical description of what happens in the worship service that Catholics call the Mass today. Note that only those in communion with the teaching of the church and who were baptized Christians were allowed to receive the Eucharist.

Irenaeus

Irenaeus was a bishop of Lyons, who was captured by the Romans and later martyred. Irenaeus was a strong defender of the faith, particularly against the Gnostics, who believed that no good could

---

[4] Ibid.

come of anything material. Thus, they believed that Jesus wasn't really incarnate, for God could not be material but must remain a spirit. They also discounted sins of the flesh—after all, it is only the spirit that matters. Sounds like modern society's view of sexual sin—if it is consensual, it is okay; it is just a physical, natural act; it doesn't affect my relationship with God; God wants me to love others. That is obviously another subject, but it does indicate where you are headed when you don't believe in the sacramental nature of Christ. Christ's body is real, and His physical act of dying on the cross did redeem man. His physical body in the Eucharist does give us His life. Let's see what Irenaeus has to say. Let's see what he died for:

> "If the Lord were from other than the Father, how could he rightly take bread, which is of the same creation as our own, and confess it to be his body and affirm that the mixture in the cup is his blood?" (Against Heresies 4:33:2 [AD 189])

> He has declared the cup, a part of creation, to be his own blood, from which he causes our blood to flow; and the bread, a part of creation, he has established as his own body, from which he gives increase unto our bodies. When, therefore, the mixed cup [wine and water] and the baked bread receives the Word of God and becomes the Eucharist, the body of Christ, and from these the substance of our flesh is increased and supported, how can they say that the flesh is not capable of receiving the gift of God, which is eternal life–flesh which is

nourished by the body and blood of the Lord, and is in fact a member of him? (Against Heresies 5:2:2–3 [AD 189])[5]

Other Early Church Fathers

The writings of the Early Church Fathers about the Eucharist are quite extensive and go beyond the scope of this book. For brevity sake, in this section I have presented snippets of writings from a variety of Early Church Fathers to help you realize how important this topic must have been to the early church.

St. John Chrysostom

"It is not man that causes the things offered to become the Body and Blood of Christ, but he who was crucified for us, Christ himself. The priest, in the role of Christ, pronounces these words, but their power and grace are God's. This is my body, he says. This word transforms the things offered."[6]

St. Ambrose of Milan

"Be convinced that this is not what nature has formed, but what the blessing has consecrated. The power of the blessing prevails over that of nature, because by the blessing nature itself has changed ... Could not Christ's word, which can make from

---

[5] Ibid, p. 294.

[6] CCC 1375.

nothing what did not exist, change existing things to what they were not before? It is no less a feat to give things their original nature than to change their nature."[7]

Clement of Alexandria

"'Eat my flesh,' [Jesus] says, 'and drink my blood.' The Lord supplies us with these intimate nutrients, he delivers over his flesh and pours out his blood, and nothing is lacking for the growth of his children" (The Instructor of Children, 1:6:43:3 [AD 191]).[8]

Tertullian

> [T]here is not a soul that can at all procure salvation, except it believe whilst it is in the flesh, so true is it that the flesh is the very condition on which salvation hinges. And since the soul is, in consequence of its salvation, chosen to the service of God, it is the flesh which actually renders it capable of such service. The flesh, indeed, is washed [in baptism], in order that the soul may be cleansed ... the flesh is shadowed with the imposition of hands [in confirmation], that the soul also may be illuminated by the Spirit; the flesh feeds [in the Eucharist] on the body and blood of Christ, that the soul likewise may be filled with God. (The Resurrection of

---

[7] CCC 1375.

[8] Cited in Jimmy Akin, *The Fathers Know Best* (El Cajon, CA: Catholic Answers, Inc., 2010), 294.

the Dead 8 [AD 210])[9]

Hippolytus

"'And she [Wisdom] has furnished her table' [Proverbs 9:2] ... refers to his [Christ's] honored and undefiled body and blood, which day by day are administered and offered sacrificially at the spiritual divine table, as a memorial of that first and ever-memorable table of the spiritual divine supper [i.e., the Last Supper]" (Fragment from Commentary on Proverbs [AD 217]).[10]

Origin of Alexandria

"Formerly there was baptism in an obscure way ... now, however, in full view, there is regeneration in water and in the Holy Spirit. Formerly, in an obscure way, there was manna for food; now, however, in full view, there is the true food, the flesh of the Word of God, as he himself says: 'My flesh is true food, and my blood is true drink' [John 6:56]" (Homilies on Numbers 7:2 [AD 248]).[11]

Cyprian of Carthage

He [Paul] threatens, moreover, the stubborn and forward, and denounces them, saying, "Whosoever eats the bread or drinks the cup of the Lord unworthily, is

---

[9] Ibid.

[10] Ibid, p. 295.

[11] Ibid.

guilty of the body and blood of the Lord" [1 Corinthians 11:27]. All these warnings being scorned and condemned before their sin is expiated, before confession has been made of their crime, before their conscience has been purged by sacrifice and by the hand of the priest, before the offense of an angry and threatening Lord has been appeased, [and so] violence is done to his body and blood; and they sin now against their Lord more with their hand and mouth than when they denied their Lord. (The Lapsed 15–16 [AD 251])[12]

Council of Nicaea I

"It has come to the knowledge of the holy and great synod that, in some districts and cities, the deacons administer the Eucharist to the presbyters [i.e., priests], whereas neither canon nor custom permits that they who have no right to offer [the Eucharistic sacrifice] should give the Body of Christ to them that do offer [it]" (Canon 18 [AD 325]).[13]

Aphrahat, the Persian Sage

"After having spoken thus [at the Last Supper], the Lord rose up from the place where he had made the Passover and had given his body as food and his blood as drink, and he went with his disciples to the place where he was to be arrested. But he ate of his own body

---

[12] Ibid.

[13] Ibid.

and drank of his own blood, while he was pondering on the dead. With his own hands the Lord presented his own body to be eaten, and before he was crucified he gave his blood as drink" (Treatises 12:6 [AD 340]).[14]

Cyril of Jerusalem

"The bread and the wine of the Eucharist before the holy invocation of the adorable Trinity were simple bread and wine, but the invocation having been made, the bread becomes the body of Christ and the wine the blood of Christ" (Catechetical Lectures 19:7 [AD 350]).

> Do not, therefore, regard the bread and wine as simply that; for they are, according to the Master's declaration, the body and blood of Christ. Even though the senses suggest to you the other, let faith make you firm. Do not judge in this matter by taste, but be fully assured by the faith, not doubting that you have been deemed worthy of the body and blood of Christ ... [Since you are] fully convinced that the apparent bread is not bread, even though it is sensible to the taste, but the body of Christ, and that the apparent wine is not wine, even though the taste would have it so, ... partake of that bread as something spiritual, and put a cheerful face on your soul. (Ibid., 22:6, 9)[15]

---

[14] Ibid, p. 296.

[15] Ibid.

St. Ambrose of Milan

"Perhaps you may be saying, 'I see something else; how can you assure me that I am receiving the body of Christ?' It but remains for us to prove it. And how many are the examples we might use! … Christ is in that sacrament, because it is the body of Christ" (The Mysteries 9:50, 58 [AD 390]).[16]

Theodore of Mopsuestia

> When [Christ] gave the bread he did not say, "This is the symbol of my body," but, "This is my body." In the same way, when he gave the cup of his blood he did not say, "This is the symbol of my blood," but, "This is my blood"; for he wanted us to look upon the [Eucharistic elements] after their reception of grace and the coming of the Holy Spirit not according to their nature, but receive them as they are, the body and blood of our Lord. We ought … not regard [the elements] merely as bread and cup, but as the body and blood of the Lord, into which they were transformed by the descent of the Holy Spirit. (Catechetical Homilies 5:1 [AD 405])[17]

Augustine of Hippo

"Christ was carried in his own hands when, referring to his own

---

[16] Ibid, p. 297.

[17] Ibid.

body, he said, 'This is my body' [Matthew 26:26]. For he carried that body in his hands" (Explanations of the Psalms 33:1:10 [AD 405]).

"I promised you [new Christians], who have now been baptized, a sermon in which I would explain the sacrament of the Lord's Table ... That bread which you see on the altar, having been sanctified by the word of God, is the body of Christ. That chalice, or rather, what is in that chalice, having been sanctified by the word of God, is the blood of Christ" (Sermons 227 [AD 411]).

"What you see is the bread and the chalice; that is what your own eyes report to you. But what your faith obliges you to accept is that the bread is the body of Christ and the chalice is the blood of Christ. This has been said very briefly, which may perhaps be sufficient for faith; yet faith does not desire instruction" (Ibid., 272).[18]

Council of Ephesus

> We will necessarily add this also. Proclaiming the death, according to the flesh, of the only-begotten Son of God, that is Jesus Christ, confessing his resurrection from the dead, and his ascension into heaven, we offer the unbloody sacrifice in the churches, and so go on to the mystical thanksgivings, and are sanctified, having received his holy flesh and the precious blood of Christ

---

[18] Ibid.

the Savior of us all. And not as common flesh do we receive it; God forbid: nor as of a man sanctified and associated with the Word according to the unity of worth, or as having a divine indwelling, but as truly the life-giving and very flesh of the Word himself. For he is the life according to his nature as God, and when he became united to his flesh, he made it also to be life-giving. (Session 1, Letter of Cyril to Nestorius [AD 431])[19]

Other Insights from Nonbelievers in the Real Presence

Believers in the Real Presence are not the only ones who have studied the Early Church Fathers; scholars who do not believe in the Real Presence have studied them as well. To see if we are misinterpreting the Early Church Fathers' writings, let's look at the analysis of a well-known twentieth-century Protestant historian from Oxford University, J. N. D. Kelly (1909–1997). Here is what J. N. D. Kelly wrote:

Eucharistic teaching, it should be understood at the outset, was in general unquestioningly realist, i.e., the consecrated bread and wine were taken to be, and were treated and designated as, the Savior's body and blood ...

The Eucharist was regarded as the distinctively

---

[19] Ibid, p. 298.

Christian sacrifice ... Malachi's prediction (1:10–11) that the Lord would reject Jewish sacrifices and instead would have "a pure offering" made to him by the Gentiles in every place was seized upon by Christians as a prophecy of the Eucharist. The Didache indeed actually applies the term thusia, or sacrifice, to the Eucharist ...

It was natural for early Christians to think of the Eucharist as a sacrifice. The fulfillment of prophecy demanded a solemn Christian offering, and the rite itself was wrapped in the sacrificial atmosphere with which our Lord invested the Last Supper. The words of institution, "Do this" (touto poieite), must have been charged with sacrificial overtones for second-century ears; Justin at any rate understood them to mean, "Offer this." ... The bread and wine, moreover, are offered "for a memorial (eis anamnasin) of the passion," a phrase which in view of his identification of them with the Lord's body and blood implies much more than an act of purely spiritual recollection.[20]

Thus, according to J. N. D. Kelly, the Early Church Fathers taught the Real Presence in the Eucharist. Many Christians do not know this to be the case. Perhaps those who do but don't believe in the Real Presence just believe that the early Christian teaching

[20] J. N. D. Kelly, *Early Christian Doctrines*, rev. ed. (New York: HarperOne, 1978), 196–197.

was in error, or that the early Christians, who were much closer to Christ and His teaching than we are, somehow never fully understood, or that perhaps modern man is more intelligent. I find that hard to believe. One only has to go to the writings of the Greeks and other civilizations to see the intelligence of those living in earlier ages. The major issue in all this is the thought that we can interpret scriptures ourselves through our own personal inspiration of the Holy Spirit. This is the so-called doctrine of perspicuity. Even if the whole of scripture were to be exhaustively researched, there would still be differences of opinion, as seen by the more than thirty thousand denominations that exist in Christianity today. On the other hand, we have the example of the Early Church Fathers to guide us to what the teachings of Christ meant to the early church. Concerning the Eucharist, as J. N. D. Kelly points out, the writings of the Early Church Fathers are undeniably realist in regard to the Eucharist. They believed the Eucharist truly was the body and blood of Jesus. I believe, as Paul taught, that the church is "the pillar and foundation of truth," and that certainly would have included the early church. Who am I, two thousand years later, to dispute it?

Perhaps another thought is that the writings we have of the Early Church Fathers really don't correspond to the church that Jesus founded. There could have been other churches that taught only the symbolic sense of the Eucharist. But who are these others? One group is the Gnostics, who believed that Jesus was not a man; they died out. Another group, the Arians, believed that Jesus was not God, only man; they died out. Jesus promised Peter that His church would not die out. It would go on and on and on. At one point during the Arian heresy, it is estimated that 75–80 percent of the church clergy taught that Jesus was only a man. But truth prevailed. In spite of some of the individual teachings or actions of the church's clergy or laity, the official teaching of the church must always remain true. Christ said it would be so when He promised to send the Spirit to guide the church. The teaching on the Eucharist is one such constant teaching. From the apostles onward, that truth has been taught. There cannot be contradictory truth. Something cannot be true and untrue at the same time.

So look at the evidence. Is it consistent? Has it always been taught? Yes, it has! Look at the consistency in the story from the Old Testament, through the Gospels, through the writings of the apostles, through the practice of the early church. Everything points to the same truth. You may say, "I know what you've said, but my eyes still tell me it is only a thin wafer of bread; it is only a cup of wine. I can't get beyond that." Remember. there are already so many irrational things in which we believe. We believe because they are true, not because they make sense. *Crede, ut intelligas—* "Believe so you may understand" (St. Augustine). Now look at the cross! Could that really be God? That man is so weak, bloody, and dirty, and He is dying. He's naked. He's suffering. Surely that can't be God. Your eyes may tell you that it cannot be true. Yet as Christians, we believe. We believe because we have seen the consistency in the story from the Old Testament, through the Gospels, through the writings of the apostles, through the teachings of the church, down through to the modern day. Simply put, it takes a faith built upon reason. Because of the consistency, my reason tells me the story of Christ—the story of the Eucharist—

is worthy of belief.
End of Chapter 6

Questions for Discussion

1) In the 4th century Arius convinced up to 80% of the bishops at that time that Jesus was not God and did not exist for all time. This was corrected over a period of time over three centuries by a number of councils beginning with the Council of Nicaea (AD 325) though the 3rd council of Constantinople (AD 680). Can you name any period in Church history, where the Church said the Eucharist was not the Body and Blood of Jesus Christ?

2) The belief in the Real Presence was not localized to one area of the Roman Empire. What modern day countries are represented by the Early Church Fathers?

Chapter 7

Just What Is the Eucharist Anyway?

How We Got to Transubstantiation

I t would be nice if the apostles would have proclaimed all the truths of the faith from the very beginning. But that is not the case and is not even possible, as God, who is the object of our faith, is infinite in His nature. Instead, as questions, misunderstandings, and/or heresies arose, the church's bishops, who succeeded the apostles, and others would meet together in councils in order to determine true doctrines consistent with the teachings of Jesus. Thus, we see that in the fourth century, the Arian heresy arose. The heresy stated that Jesus was not God. This resulted in great discussions among the church hierarchy that needed to be resolved. This discernment as to who Jesus really is took place over three centuries and involved a number of church councils, beginning with the first council of Niceae in AD 325, through the third council of Constantinople in AD 680. At these councils, among other items, it was determined that Jesus was both God and man, that he had a divine and a human nature (hypostatic union), that God is a Trinity, that Mary was truly *theotokos*—the Mother of God, and that Jesus has both a divine will and a human will (but the human will was always aligned with the divine). The church, however, did not make up these doctrines. The doctrines at that time flowed from past teaching. The doctrines were present in the past but were never fully articulated, because … well, there was no great reason to. This is true of many of the church's dogmas and doctrines. They came to be fully explained (under the guidance of the Holy Spirit) when there came a need to be explained.

The doctrine of the Eucharist is no different. From scripture and the writings of the church, it is obvious that from the beginning of Christianity, not all believed or properly understood what the Eucharist is, as taught by the church. To show this, let me give you two examples and refer you to Paul in 1 Corinthians 11:29, where he states, "For anyone who eats and drinks without discerning the body eats and drinks judgment upon himself," and to the quote of Ignatius of Antioch to the Smyrnaeans, where Ignatius states, "They abstain from the Eucharist and from prayer because they do not confess that the Eucharist is the flesh of our Savior Jesus Christ." Obviously, Paul and Ignatius wrote the verses because there was a misunderstanding or a dissension about what the Eucharist was.

No one should be surprised by this. The Eucharist has always been "a hard teaching" (John 6:60), a flashpoint for dissent, beginning from that very first day when Jesus spoke about eating His body and drinking His blood in John 6. The church, as a body, has always taught that the Eucharist is the body and blood of our Lord Jesus Christ. What is really amazing, though, considering the differing opinions of various Christian groups in the present day, is the lack of any dissent among the writings of the Early Church Fathers or of the Catholic Church Magisterium. Surely, one might say, somebody must have taught that the Eucharist was just symbolic. But the answer is that there was no church father who said otherwise, although there are those who have believed that Augustine might have thought so. It is important to clear up this loose end so you understand what Augustine was really saying— and so you don't think I am just whitewashing the discussion and avoiding any negative commentary. So let's look at some of Augustine writings, which at first seem to be in conflict.

Augustine

Unquestionably, Augustine documents that the reception of Eucharist was a routine weekly or even daily event, and certainly, he seemed to be solidly behind the teaching that the Eucharist is truly the body and blood of Jesus.[1] Augustine sums up these points thus: "Some receive the Body and Blood of the Lord every day; others on certain days; in some places there is no day on which the Sacrifice is not offered; in others on Saturday and Sunday only; in others on Sunday alone."[2] However, some of his writings do seem to present the possibility of a symbolic interpretation. In "On Christian Doctrine,"[3] he states, "The Lord

---

[1] James O'Connor, *The Hidden Manna*, 2nd ed. (San Francisco: Ignatius Press, 2005), 49.

[2] Thomas Scannell, "Frequent Communion," *The Catholic Encyclopedia*, vol. 6 (New York: Robert Appleton Company, 1909). Accessed 6 Jan. 2014, http://www.newadvent.org/cathen/06278a.htm.

[3] Christina De Doctrina, 55; CSEL 80 (Corpus Scriptorum ecclesiaticorum latinorum, Vienna, 1866–), 93–94.

says, 'Unless you eat the Flesh of the Son of Man and drink His blood, you will not have life in you.' This appears to order us to do something disgraceful or evil. Therefore, it is symbolic, command-ing us to communicate in the Passion of the Lord and to remember pleasantly and usefully that the flesh was crucified and wounded for us." In another writing, this one a commentary on Psalm 3, he speaks of "the banquet in which the Lord entrusted and handed over to the disciples the symbol of his Body and Blood."[4]

Well, I guess that is the end of this book! A nonbeliever in the Real Presence might say, "See? Augustine said it is symbolic. If Augustine said it, I believe it." However, this would be a very unfair assessment of the situation. First of all, no one has said that Augustine was infallible in his teaching. Jesus promised the apostles that He would send the Holy Spirit to lead them into truth, not to each individual bishop. This promise of Christ—that what is taught is true—applies only to what the church teaches concerning faith and morals. The promise would not apply to a teaching unrelated to faith and morals. As a result, the church may support or disregard any one theologian's teaching or any part thereof. Augustine could be wrong and, in fact, later in life, he did correct some of the misconceptions he made earlier along the way. Second, there is context and the question of philology—what did the words mean to Augustine, and how did he use the words? Were these words consistent with his other teachings?

Here are two other quotes from Augustine. In a sermon to those who had just been baptized, Augustine says, "That bread you see on the altar and that has been sanctified by the word of God is the Body of Christ. That chalice—rather, that which the chalice contains, is the Blood of Christ. Through these things the Lord Jesus Christ wished us his Body and his Blood, *which he shed for us unto the remission of sins*. If you receive them well, you are that which you receive" (italics added).[5] And elsewhere, he states, "We did not know him in the flesh, yet we have deserved to eat his flesh and to be his members in his Flesh."[6] This directly states that Christians, though they have never met Jesus directly, do eat His flesh.

So what is going on? Was Augustine just a politician who told groups whatever he thought they might like to hear, or did he just like to contradict himself? *Or* is there something in the meaning of the ancient texts that we misunderstand? It turns out that Augustine used the term sacrament differently from theologians of our day. As shown by James O'Connor in his book *The Hidden Manna*, Augustine's reference to sacrament often refers to the visible element of the sacrament, that which we now term the *sacramentum tantum.*[7] The visible element does have a sacramental, symbolic value. The starting point of every sacrament is its *sacramentum tantum*. For instance, water is used in baptism. Water does have significant symbolic value; for instance, it

---

[5] Augustine, Sermon 227: On Easter Sunday; PL 38 (Patrino Latina Migne, Paris, 1878–1890).

[6] Augustine, In Johannis Evan., 31, 11, p. 299.

[7] James O'Connor, *The Hidden Manna*, 2nd ed. (San Francisco: Ignatius Press, 2005), 55.

cleanses, can cause death, and is necessary for life. Combined with the Trinitarian baptismal words, the person baptized truly is correspondingly purified, dies to his past self, and receives supernatural life. Jesus chose bread and wine to be the *sacramentum tantum* of the Eucharist. Bread and wine, which give our bodies life-sustaining sustenance and are works of human hands, are to be offered to the Father. There is also a natural symbolism in the reception of bread and wine. The use of bread and wine symbolizes what is going on. However, to truly give eternal life and to be offered to the Father for our salvation, the bread and wine must change into true flesh and blood and be the very flesh that hung on the tree of Calvary. The Eucharist truly represents Calvary and the sacrificial offering in an unbloody manner. The bread and wine as *sacramentum tantum* is symbolic; what it becomes is not.

Did others of Augustine's time understand the Eucharist as really the body and blood of Christ? Theodore of Mopsuestia, bishop of Mopsuestia (modern Yakapinar) from AD 392 to 428, put it this way: "It is with justice, therefore, that when he gave the bread he did not say, 'This is the symbol of my Body.'"[8] This sounds like many Catholic apologists I have heard discuss the Eucharist. It even sounds similar to one minister I heard on a radio talk show, except that she warned her listeners that what Jesus meant when He said, "This is my body," was "This is like my body." Of course, by adding to the scriptures, she got it exactly backward from what the New Testament writers believed and the

---

[8] Ibid, p. 69.

Early Church Fathers taught.

Formulating the Teaching

Academics can be a wonderful thing. Through academics, concepts can be developed, insight gained, and understanding passed on to others. But it is not always a smooth process. Often, the very act of writing a paper or a book can invoke great controversy and "stir the waters." But eventually, the truth generally appears; that is, assuming the truth is knowable. So it was for the church concerning the Eucharist. Around AD 831, Paschasius Radbertus (circa AD 785–859) wrote a theological monograph titled "De Corpore et Sanguine Domini"; that is, "The Body and Blood of the Lord." In this monograph, the future St. Radbertus attempts to put into writing the beliefs of the church concerning the Eucharist, as taught since the time of the apostles. The titles of some of his chapters are revealing.[9]

> Chapter 1: "It is not to be doubted that the Eucharist is the True Body and Blood of Christ"
> Chapter 2: "What are Sacraments?"
> Chapter 3: "Whether This Mystery in Chalice Becomes a Sacrament in Figure or in Reality"
> Chapter 4: "Whether this Mystery of the Chalice Becomes a Sacrament in Figure or in Reality"

---

[9] CCCM (Corpus Christianorum Continatio Mediaevalis), vol. 16 (Belgium: Turnhout, 1953).

Chapter 7: "In What Ways the Body of Christ Is Spoken Of"[10]

His sentiments on the reality of the body and blood of the Lord in the Eucharist can be found in a few quotes:

> "[The Eucharist is] clearly no other flesh than that which was born of Mary, suffered on the cross, and rose from the tomb."[11]

> "If [one] should see Christ on the cross in the appearance of a slave, how would he know him to be God unless he had first believed through Faith."[12] (And I thought this was a modern-day apologetic!)

> "So as True Flesh was created ... without intercourse, so the same Body and Blood ... might be mystically created from bread and wine."[13]

True to life, the monograph did not put to rest all the enigmas and questions concerning the Eucharist. As is typical, suddenly many theologians felt called to add, subtract, nuance, and expand their thoughts on the Eucharist. Probably most significant are the

---

[10] CCCM (Corpus Christianorum Continatio Mediaevalis), vol. 16 (Belgium: Turnhout, 1953).

[11] Paschasius Radbertus, *De Corpore et Sanguine Domini,* I, 45-52,PP14-15, as cited in James O'Connor, *The Hidden Manna,* 2nd ed. (San Francisco: Ignatius Press, 2005), 86.

[12] Ibid.

[13] Ibid, p. 87.

writings of Ratramnus of Corbie, who responded to the monograph with a book of the same title. He stated that the Eucharist received from the church is not the same as the body and blood born to Mary but is the body and blood of Jesus in figure. He states, "In appearance it is bread. In Sacrament it is the Body and Blood of Christ." [14] This seemingly is a different teaching compared to that of Radbertus. Since Radbertus was an abbot at the same abbey as Ratramnus, there must have been interesting dinner conversations and perhaps even food fights between the two of them! However, there is no evidence of even a rift between them. If we apply the same *sacramentum tantum* concept to Ratramus's work as was done to some of Augustine's words, and if we recognize that "figure" is not identical to "symbol," we can see a nuance rather than a disagreement. It is difficult to determine the exact meaning of Ratramus's writing in this regard.

His book, however, would reemerge two centuries later, with John Scotus Erigena named as the author, and at that time would cause misunderstandings.

Berengarius of Tours

As expected, the topic of the Eucharist was periodically addressed over the years following St. Radbertus's work. Terminology with regard to various aspects of the Eucharist became more refined.

---

[14] Ratramus of Corbie, *De Corpore et Sanguine Domini*, 9; 121, 131, as cited in James O'Connor, *The Hidden Manna*, 2nd ed. (San Francisco: Ignatius Press, 2005), 93.

But while different aspects of the Eucharist were discussed, the Eucharist was always considered to be Christ's body and blood. However, this was to change in the eleventh century with the arrival of Berengarius of Tours.

Around AD 1040, Berengarius, a deacon, began to teach that the Eucharist was just symbolic. He based this, in part, on the work of John Scotus Erigena (who was really Paschasius Radbertus) and cited also Ambrose and Augustine, among others. Apparently, he did not recognize, agree with, or understand the *sacramentum tantum* aspect of their writings. Because of these teachings, in 1050, Berengarius eventually was brought before a synod in Rome of various bishops (including Pope Leo IX). He was asked to defend his teaching. He was unsuccessful in convincing the synod, and as a result, he was provisionally excommunicated, pending another synod, to be held later in the year. He failed to attend that synod, and his teachings were further condemned. Eventually, at a synod at Tours in 1054, Berengarius assured the bishops that after the consecration, the Eucharist really was the body and blood of Christ. He signed a document so stating, but he continued in his previous teachings.

From that time on, the question of what the Eucharist really is was raised over and over again. Because of all the synods and writings associated with the Eucharist at that time, it is clear that Berengarius had struck a nerve. Berengarius's beliefs arose, in part, due to his comparison of the Eucharist to the other sacraments. In baptism, the element of water is not changed, yet grace is transferred. In confirmation, the element of oil does not change, yet grace is transferred. Why should the bread and wine be changed in the Eucharist? The church, however, considered this teaching of Berengarius to be a new teaching, inconsistent with past teachings, which originated with the apostles and the Early Church Fathers. Therefore, the teaching was to be discontinued.

While the mechanism for this change of bread and wine into Jesus's body and blood had never been formally discussed, it is evident, based on its actions, that from the church's long-standing teaching, as seen in the writings of the Early Church Fathers, the church had always taught that with the words of consecration there is a change and that the Eucharist becomes the body and blood of Christ. Berengarius really wasn't a heretic at this point. His teaching could be looked upon as theological speculation. His teachings, however, did continue to spread, and as a result, there was confusion among the laity concerning the Eucharist.

To address this issue, the church, under Pope Nicholas II, called in 1059 yet another synod, which Berengarius did attend. The teaching again was found erroneous, and eventually, Berengarius was asked to and did submit a Profession of Faith to the church's teaching on the Eucharist. In spite of this, a year later Berengarius chose to create a pamphlet condemning the synod and the pope, while defending his own view. The church continued to make many efforts to bring Berengarius back into the fold. Around 1061, Pope Alexander II, the successor to Pope Nicholas II, wrote him an encouraging letter, while at the same time warning him to give no further offense. Pope Gregory VII (Hildebrand), Alexander II's successor, summoned Berengarius to Rome in 1078, encouraging him to sign a revised affidavit of a belief in the body and blood of Christ in the Eucharist. Berengarius did write and submit a revised affidavit, but the affidavit still allowed him to profess that the bread and wine remained as they were before the consecration.

In response to Berengarius's teaching, circa 1079, Norman Guitmund, bishop of Aversa, wrote a treatise defending the Eucharist. [15] His book contained the following important elements:

- The Eucharist is that flesh that "is that born to Mary … reigns in heaven."
- The change is "Not Comprehended by senses."
- Change of a "substance" into a preexisting body and blood of Christ.
- Calls it "transmutation."
- Same body, different form.
- "Accidents" of bread and wine remain.
- Does not hurt Jesus.

Finally, in 1080, Berengarius signed a document acknowledging the essence of transubstantiation and then retired. The church had defended its teaching on the Real Presence. It is obvious from the strong response of the church that up to this point, a symbolic Eucharist was not something to be considered part of the deposit of faith received from the apostles.

---

[15] Guitmand, De Corpori; *Patrtolinga latina*, Migne, Paris 1878–1890.

The Spirit-Guided Church Steps In

It is well known that when questions on doctrine arise, it often requires a period of years—even centuries—for the church to look closely at its teaching and to determine a proper response. Such was the case, for instance, with the Arian controversy and associated heresies. Under the guidance of the Holy Spirit, over a period of 126 years, the church, in its Council of Nicaea (AD 325), the First Council of Constantinople (AD 381), the Council of Ephesus (AD 431), and the Council of Chalcedon (AD 451) determined that God is a Trinity, Jesus was true God and true Man, Mary was the mother of God, Jesus had two natures (divine and human that were hypostatically combined), Jesus was but one person, and that Jesus had two distinct wills (but His human will is always aligned with His divine will). Later, the Third Council of Constantinople (AD 680) also confirmed these tenets.

Please remember that doctrines, such as that of the Trinity, the divine nature of Jesus, and the hypostatic union, cannot be understood on the basis of the knowledge from our senses and of human reason alone. Without the infallible guidance from the Holy Spirit on the church's teaching, it is highly unlikely that these doctrines would have been ascertained simply through an individual's personal interpretation of the scriptures. To have a correct theological understanding, one must always have the Spirit-guided teaching of the church, conjoined with the supernatural virtue of faith. To emphasis this, remember, as St. Radbertus suggested, that no one who looked at Jesus, bruised, battered, hanging on the cross at Calvary, would say, "Look—there is God!" That our human senses and reason simply cannot come to that conclusion does not make the Christian faith false. After all, if it is true, it is okay, whether or not our reason finds it to be rational. Truth is what it is. Because of the writings of scripture, the words and deeds performed by Jesus, the trueness of Jesus's message, the actions of the apostles after the apostles received the Holy Spirit on Pentecost, the continuity of church teaching (much less the continuity of the church), we, as Catholics, are able to profess and proclaim that Jesus is Lord and Savior and that we are part of his church. In other words, we take the leap of faith. So too has been the case for the Real Presence in the Eucharist. Once the heresy arose, the church, through its Spirit-guided teaching, met in councils, issued encyclicals, maintained a continuity with the past, and revealed infallibly the truth of "what is the Eucharist?" and "What is the nature of this change that takes place?"

Developing Concepts

The process was not painless along the way. Other related heresies would arrive as various sects arose. Not only would the Albigensians (twelfth and thirteenth centuries) argue that only they had the true priesthood and that Catholic Mass was therefore of no avail, but they would maintain that their own bodies were the flesh of the Lord. The Waldensians (thirteenth to sixteenth centuries, primarily) would maintain that any holy person could confect the Eucharist. Later, they would insist that Eucharist should be confected only on Holy Thursday. Individuals must have felt that the Eucharistic teaching was "up for grabs." If you could justify it, you could teach it.

Within the church a deeper, more complete understanding of the Eucharist was sought. For example, in the scholastic theology of the twelfth and thirteenth centuries, the church theologians tried to answer questions, such as:

- "Does the Eucharist change back to bread when lost?"
- "What happens if a sinner receives the host?"
- "What about a mouse who eats the host? Does it receive Jesus?"
- While not necessarily questions that would lead someone to Christ, I guess they were questions on which to speculate.

Choosing the Right Word

New terminology, or should I say old terminology, was also introduced to define the Eucharist. In the twelfth century, Pope Alexander III (AD 1105–1181) and Alan of Lille (AD 1116–1202) "resurrected" the term *transubstantiation* from Aristotelian metaphysics. For Pope Alexander III, the term was mostly a new word to employ. Alan of Lille, in his *Four Books Against Heresies*,[16] was the major proponent of the use of the term *transubstantiation* as a philosophical treatise on the change found in the Eucharist.

---

[16] Alan of Lille, *Contra Haereticos Libri Quatuor*, chap. 68; PL, 210, 360–361, as cited in James O'Connor, *The Hidden Manna*, 2nd ed. (San Francisco: Ignatius Press, 2005), 117.

For the ancient Greeks, particularly Aristotle, substance was essence; that is, "what it was to be." And from the *Stanford Encyclopedia of Philosophy* definition of substance: "'the essence of a thing is what it is said to be in respect of itself.' It is important to remember that for Aristotle, one defines things, not words. The definition of tiger does not tell us the meaning of the word tiger; it tells us what it is to be a tiger, what a tiger is said to be in respect to itself. Thus, the definition of tiger states the essence—the 'what it is to be' of a tiger, what is predicated of the tiger per se."[17] One aspect that must be discussed concerning Aristotelian metaphysics is acknowledgement that *transubstantiation* is not a biblical term. This poses a problem for "Bible only" folks, yet many concepts are not defined in the Bible. Two examples are the Trinity (three persons in one being) and the hypostatic union (the union of Jesus's human and divine nature in one person). While not in the Bible, these concepts are held by nearly all individuals who call themselves Christian. In fact, this issue of the use of nonbiblical Greek terms, such *homo-ousis*, *hypostasis*, and *prosopon*, which were used in the early church councils, was indeed brought up as an argument against the doctrines of the Trinity and the hypostatic union. Nonetheless, the concepts of Trinity and hypostasis were maintained. Similarly, in regard to use of the word

---

[17] S. Marc Cohen, "Aristotle's Metaphysics," *The Stanford Encyclopedia of Philosophy* (Summer 2012 Edition), Edward N. Zalta (ed.), http://plato.stanford.edu/archives/sum2012/entries/aristotle-metaphysics/.

transubstantiation, if a word is *the* word that best describes the process, it should be used. Just because the word was developed by Greeks and not by Israelites, that is no reason not to use it. In the end, the term *transubstantiation* was chosen by the Catholic Church as a more complete description of the process of describing the change. It was not anything new and was consistent with past teaching.

The Church Holds a Council

Eventually, the question of what the Eucharist really is was so great that it needed to be defined by an ecumenical council. This was done as part of the Fourth Lateran Council in AD 1215. The Fourth Lateran Council was held under Pope Innocent III. It was a large council, covering many topics. Present at the council were the patriarchs of Constantinople and Jerusalem, 71 archbishops, 412 bishops, and 800 abbots, the primate of the Maronites, and St. Dominic. A few other issues discussed included the Albigensians and the Trinitarian errors of Abbot Joachim. The council also published seventy important reformatory decrees. In regard to the Eucharist, it considered four possible Eucharistic processes:

Purely Symbolic:	Jesus does not exist in the bread.
Impanation:	Similar to the hypostatic union—true God and true man but would be true God and true bread/wine.

Consubstantiation:	The substance of both bread and wine would be present together with the substance of Jesus; that is, the body, blood, soul, and divinity, yet still distinct, comparable to the Trinity, where Jesus is consubstantial with the Father; Jesus is truly one with the Father, yet His personhood is distinct.
Transubstantiation:	The substance of the bread and wine are transformed into the substance of Jesus; that is, body, blood, soul, and divinity. The accidents of bread and wine remain, but bread and wine are no longer there.

Of these possibilities, the Catholic Church rejected "purely symbolic" as simply being incompatible with 1,200 years of church teaching. A symbolic Eucharist was always considered heretical. Impanation was rejected, as Jesus would be inseparably joined by nature to bread/wine. Consubstantiation was considered but was found not to be consistent with what the church had always taught. For instance, Ignatius of Antioch had taught that the Eucharist was "the Flesh of our Savior Jesus Christ, which suffered for our sins." The Catholic Church has never referred to the Eucharist as the flesh of our Savior Jesus Christ *and* true bread and wine. (True God/true man/true bread/true wine?) As difficult as it may seem to our worldly mind, the church chose transubstantiation and stated the accidents of bread and wine remain, but there is no bread and wine remaining in the consecrated host and consecrated wine. It is gone! The bread and wine is not annihilated but transformed into the flesh and blood of Jesus! The term transubstantiation correctly describes this process. A secondary miracle enables the flesh and blood to appear to keep the "accidents"; that is, the outward characteristics of bread and water.

However, even some well-known theologians favored consubstantiation. More than half a century later, John Duns Scotus (1266–1308) stated:

> I say that it is quite possible for God to have brought it about that the Body of Christ be truly present even while the substance of bread remain … [however, Transubstantiation] must be held as of the substance of the Faith because it is a solemn declaration made by the Church. And if you ask why the Church chose so difficult an understanding … I reply because that the Scriptures are expounded by the same Spirit … and the Catholic Church has expounded that Faith passed to us by the same Spirit … and has chosen this under-standing because it is true.[18]

Thus, to paraphrase the above, we believe it, because Jesus said to the apostles, "When the Spirit of truth comes, he will guide you into all the truth" (John 16:13), and thus the church is guided into

---

[18] John Duns Scotus, Quaestiones In Librium Sententiarum, IV, dist. II, q. 3, in Opera Omnia Joannis Duns Scoti, 17 (Paris: Vives, 1894), 375–376.

all the truth. Truth is always the reason we seek for belief, not whether we understand it completely or whether it agrees with our rational, senses-based understanding.

But Others Do Not Believe the Same

Not surprisingly, after every church council there is a flurry of activity by individuals who disagree with the council decisions. So too with the teaching on the Eucharist. Others would not believe, particularly those who had other disagreements with the church. John Wycliffe (1320–1384) proposed in 1380 a virtual presence and declared, as an individual, that the teachings of consubstantiation and transubstantiation were heretical. For him, the Eucharist was a shadowy figure, a spiritual figure of Jesus Christ. Jesus is not there bodily, nor is He there in sign only, but "in more efficaciously than a sign."[19] Jesus exists but not in a substantive way. Because Jesus was not truly there, Wycliffe was also against Eucharistic adoration. He acknowledged the fact that the faithful in the church believed in the Real Presence, but he felt that he, being a trained theologian, was superior to the *"sensus fidelium"* (sense of the faithful), for they were too unintelligent to know what to believe.[20] Wycliffe's views were rejected by various synods in England, but he was never excommunicated, dying in his own parish in 1384.

---

[19] Wycliffe, *De Eucharistia*, ch. 4, 121.

[20] James O'Connor, *The Hidden Manna*, 2nd ed. (San Francisco: Ignatius Press, 2005), 128.

But dissent was in vogue, and there would be many Eucharistic heresies to follow. With the Reformation, Martin Luther taught that transubstantiation was false and what came to later be called consubstantiation was true. He did, however, believe in the Real Presence but that the miracle only occurred during the service. Taking the Eucharist to the sick or worshipping the Eucharist at a later time was of no avail. Also, he did not believe the Eucharist was a representation of the Paschal sacrifice.

To Luther's chagrin, other leaders in the Reformation did not agree with his views of the Eucharist. John Calvin (1509–1564) believed that the Eucharist was purely a relationship, and that pure bread and wine no longer existed. Those who receive the elements with faith can receive the actual body and blood of Christ through the power of the Holy Spirit that works through the sacrament, a view sometimes known as *receptionism*.

Calvin explains it this way:

> They could never have been so foully deluded by Satan's tricks unless they had been bewitched by this error [i.e., transubstantiation], that Christ's body, enclosed in bread, is transmitted by mouth into the stomach. The cause of such crude imagination was that among consecration was virtually equivalent to magic incantation. But this principle was hidden from them, that the bread is a sacrament only to those persons to whom the word is directed; just as the water of baptism is not changed in itself, but as soon as the promise has been

attached it begins to be for us what it was not before.[21]

Perhaps one of the reasons why Calvin thought that all of the early and medieval church was deluded by Satan's tricks was that he didn't have access to the writings of many of the Early Church Fathers, as we do today, and he couldn't see the consistency in the church's teachings since day one. Having the belief that Jesus is not truly present as a substance, Calvin necessarily was against adoration, and, like Luther, he did not believe the Eucharist to be a representation of the Paschal sacrifice.

In 1533, King Henry VIII of England—in part because he was refused an annulment of his marriage to Queen Catherine—separated from the Catholic Church and declared himself head of the Church of England (the Anglican Church). Prior to that time, Henry VIII had strong Catholic beliefs and even was named Defender of the Faith by Pope Leo X in 1521. Soon after, however, the Anglican Church was formed and split from the Catholic Church. Subsequently, the Anglican Church developed a Calvinistic tradition that at one point, during the period of the Commonwealth from 1649 to 1660, removed all bishops from the church, only to have them later restored with the return of the monarchy. During the time of no bishops, the Eucharist was simply viewed as more or less a symbolic view of the Eucharist. The following is an official statement of the Church of England, written in 1571, as found in its Articles of Religion:

---

[21] John Calvin, *Institutes*, bk IV, chap 17, 14, p. 1,376.

"Transubstantiation (or the change of the substance of
Bread and Wine) in the Supper of the Lord, cannot be
proved by Holy Writ; but is repugnant to the plain
words of Scripture, overthroweth the nature of a
Sacrament, and hath given occasion to many
superstitions."[22]

In another variation, Ulrich Zwingli had no regard for any
sacramental nature of the Eucharist and proposed what is now
known as *memorialism*. In this view, the Lord's supper is simply a
remembrance of Christ's suffering and a reminder of Jesus's power
to overcome sin and death. There is no grace inherent in the bread
and wine. Grace may be obtained through prayerful thoughts and
reflections of what Jesus has done for us. This is the view of most
Baptists, Evangelicals, and non-denominationals today.

As the last and most opposite extreme of transubstantiation,
groups such as Quakers and the Salvation Army do not practice
any observance of the Eucharist.

The Council of Trent to the Present

With the Protestant Reformation in full force, the Catholic Church
had much to respond to in regard to many of its teachings,
including the beliefs concerning the Eucharist. As part of the
Council of Trent (intermittently held in five sessions between 1545
and 1563), the church reconfirmed its belief in transubstantiation,
that bread/wine no longer exists, our senses are fooled, that the

---

[22] Articles of Religion, Church of England, Art. 28 (1571).

Eucharist becomes the body and blood of Jesus independent of the state of the priest or the receiver, and that it remains the body and blood of Jesus even after the Mass and therefore can be taken to the sick, adored, and must be stored appropriately. Furthermore, the Mass is the same sacrifice as at Calvary.[23]

Trent quelled most of the discussion within the Catholic Church concerning the Eucharist, but theological speculation was still advanced by various Catholic theologians who continued to want to redefine the Eucharist. In the twentieth century there arose the concepts of *transignification* and *transfinalization*. Transignification states that at the consecration in the Mass, the bread and wine take on the significance of Jesus's body and blood. Transfinalization states that, at the consecration in the Mass, the bread and wine take on a new function of Jesus's body and blood. These interpretations were condemned by Pope Paul VI in the encyclical *Mysterium Fidei* (1995).

And what are the modern beliefs of the Anglicans, the Orthodox, and many Lutherans? Eventually, the Church of England became worldwide and formed the Anglican Communion of Churches. The Anglican Communion came to hold three traditions: the Evangelical, Catholic, and Liberal traditions, of which only the Catholic tradition retains a concept of the Eucharist as a true sacrament. Currently, most of the Anglican Communion believe what is sometimes referred to as moderate realism—"Christ is truly present and received without

---

23   http://www.catholicliturgy.com/index.cfm/FuseAction/DocumentContents/DocumentIndex/502.

any change in the substance of the bread and wine of the Eucharist." [24] What is somewhat revealing is that within the Anglican Church, one can believe whatever one wants—symbolic, undefined Real Presence (moderate realism, as above), or transubstantiation, depending on which tradition the individual chooses to believe.

I haven't previously addressed the belief of the Orthodox (Greek, Russian, etc.) but need to now. The Orthodox churches separated from the Roman Catholic Church in 1054 in a dispute unrelated to the Eucharist. As such, the Orthodox do believe in the Real Presence but do not use the term *transubstantiation*. Orthodox and many Lutherans now prefer to believe in the objective reality but maintain pious silence about technicalities.

Reflection

There is a wide range of beliefs here. It is as if the first fifteen centuries of belief in the Real Presence was for naught. It is as if the famous words of the refrain to the hymn "Faith of Our Fathers" [25]—"Faith of our fathers, holy faith! We will be true to thee till death," which are sung by many nonbelievers in the Real Presence—apply only to a relatively few generations, not back to the Early Church Fathers.

---

[24] http://anglicaneucharistictheology.com/Anglican_Eucharistic_Theology/Case_Studies/Entries/2006/1/25_Anglican-Roman_Catholic_International_Commission_(ARCIC).html.

[25] http://en.wikipedia.org/wiki/Faith_of_Our_Fathers_(hymn).

Much of the concern of those groups who do not believe in the Real Presence seems to be associated with the thought that the Eucharist just doesn't look like the body and blood of Jesus. For instance, Calvin speaks of "Satan's tricks." In another words, it seems irrational, and a memorialization or spiritual presence seems easier to believe. It is not whether the Real Presence is rational but rather that it is true. Certainly, these faiths already believe that transubstantiation can occur, because they believe in the miracle of Cana. Personally, I believe the following reasons already discussed for accepting the Real Presence all are consistent with the Real Presence and give a preponderance of evidence for belief:

- Old Testament foreshadowing the words and actions of the New Testament
- the consistency of the teaching of the Apostolic and post-Apostolic fathers and of the Magisterium

Yet that may not be enough evidence for others. Fortunately, God has given us even more concrete evidence of the truth of the Real Presence: the doctrinal miracles. Let's examine these miracles.

End of Chapter 7

Questions for Discussion

1) This chapter discussed the *sacramentum tantum* of Baptism and of the Eucharist. What would be the various *sacramentum tantum* of the sacrament of Marriage, the sacrament of Confirmation (or Chrismation), the sacrament of Reconciliation, the sacrament of Holy Orders, and the sacrament of Anointing of the Sick?

The various beliefs found in Christianity concerning the Eucharist belies the one aspect lacking in all non-Catholic Christian churches. What is that aspect?

Chapter 8

God's Verification

The Doctrinal Eucharistic Miracles

J esus promised to send the Holy Spirit to lead the church in truth, and so we believe the church has been led to the truth by its councils, encyclicals, and through its interpretations found in its sacred tradition. But knowing how difficult it is for some to accept the Real Presence in the Eucharist, has God done anything else to help our unbelief? Remember the story in Mark 9 of the father with the son possessed by a spirit. The father wants Jesus to help him and his son, and he asks Jesus for help, adding the following words: "if you can." Jesus is perhaps incredulous; after all, how many spirits does Jesus have to cast out before someone will believe it is within His power? He replies, "If you can! All things are possible to him who believes." The man responds, "I believe. Help my unbelief" (Mark 9:14–24). Jesus then heals the boy. Aren't we all like that man? If only I would see an instantaneous, unquestionable miracle, I would believe 110 percent.

This is a common problem. I can't tell you how many times someone has asked me whether I believe that miracles still occur. Many people just do not believe that miracles are still possible in this day and age. But if you think about it, wouldn't it be strange if miracles *didn't* still occur? To believe that, we would have to join those Deists who believe God created the world and its occupants and then stepped back and said, "Go to it, humans! I'll see you when you die." If this were the case, what would have been the reason for creating man? Why would God have performed miracles in the past and then suddenly quit, just because the apostles died off? Did God change? No, I seem to remember that God doesn't change. If God was willing to perform miracles before the "cultural event," I am sure He is willing to perform miracles after the cultural event.

So, is there anything that God might have done or still does in order to help our unbelief in regard to accepting the Real Presence in the consecrated bread and wine? Well, the answer is *yes*! God has given us Eucharistic miracles that are doctrinal in nature; that is, they demonstrate that the teaching of the church on the Real Presence is true. Eucharistic miracles are miracles in which, in some cases, a consecrated host turns into real flesh and consecrated wine turns into real blood. God has given us other miracles as well—miracles of dramatic healing, miracles demonstrating that events such as Fatima are true, miracles of protection, miracles overriding nature. I realize some miracles have been faked by unprincipled people, and this tends to cast doubt as to the reality of God's miracles. So in order to bolster our belief in the Real Presence, I will describe a couple of miracles associated with the reality of the Real Presence. These miracles reveal that the consecrated bread and wine truly are flesh and blood. However, to counteract the residual effects of shyster "miracles," my examples are not legendary stories but are ones that can be viewed and investigated today. These miracles are ongoing, in spite of the fact that the miracle may have originally occurred centuries ago. Because they physically exist today, one cannot dismiss them.

The Eucharistic Miracle of Lanciano, Italy, in the Eighth Century

This miracle is perhaps the most famous Eucharistic miracle. A full accounting of the miracle can be found in numerous texts.[1] The account goes as follows: Around AD 700, a Basilian monk (an order of St. Basil the Great, who lived from AD 329 to 379) was having severe doubts as to the reality of the bread and wine changing into the body and blood of Jesus in the Eucharist. In spite of his doubt, he continued to say Mass as usual at the Church of St. Longinus in Lanciano, Italy. Suddenly, after the consecration of the hosts and the wine, the "accidents" of the bread changed into both "accidents" of bread and of flesh (which I will refer to as bread and flesh for ease in presenting the account). The very outer edge of the host remained bread, while the flesh became very thick at the outer edge and then thinned out near the center.

This would be miraculous enough, but it would be just a good story, if not for the *fact* that the miraculous host and blood are still around today and available to be analyzed. And analyzed, it has

---

[1] See, for instance, *Eucharistic Miracles* by Joan Cruz, or *The Eucharistic Miracles of the World* by the Institute of St. Clement I, Pope and Martyr. These books are listed in the "Suggested Reading" section at the end of the book.

been. These elements have been exposed to air and have not been chemically treated for 1,300 years, yet they still exist.

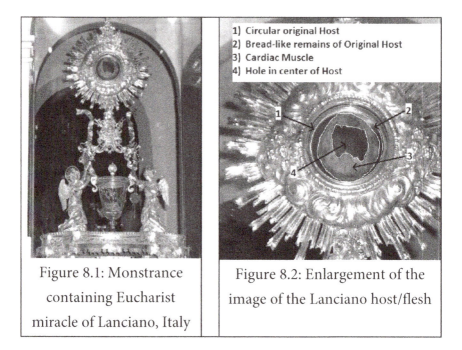

| Figure 8.1: Monstrance containing Eucharist miracle of Lanciano, Italy | Figure 8.2: Enlargement of the image of the Lanciano host/flesh |

Bread, tissue, wine, and blood decay with time, so the fact that these elements exist today is a phenomenon in itself. The host/flesh remains the same as it was on the day the miracle occurred, except that the thin center portion of bread has disappeared. The blood has now coagulated into five separate pellets. In 1970, Dr. Odoardo Linoli, a professor of anatomy and pathological histology in chemistry and in clinical microscopy in Arezzo, Italy, examined the elements. The tissue and the blood are similar to any biopsy material obtained from an operating room, which one would send to a pathologist for examination. In effect, when tested, the tissue and blood act as if they had just been removed from a living person.

The tissue type is striated muscular heart tissue from the myocardium (heart wall), from the left ventricle. The tissue is human and contains arteries and veins, along with the vagus nerve. The blood type is AB (about 6 percent of people have type AB blood). The blood comes from a man of Middle Eastern origin. These results were published in a peer-reviewed journal[2] and later verified in 1973 by a scientific commission appointed by the chief advisory board of the World Health Organization. All in all, their testing lasted fifteen months and included more than five hundred tests. The results were consistent with the 1970 tests. Don't believe the tests? Go and see it for yourself, as I did in the summer of 2014. It is available for daily viewing. In fact, they even have street signs to show you the way.

There is no rational explanation for the host or the coagulated pellets. In all aspects, the miracle of Lanciano certainly does exemplify the doctrine of transubstantiation, as upon the saying of the words of consecration by a priest, the bread and wine became flesh and blood. While no one can say that this heart muscle and blood sample are truly the heart muscle and blood of Jesus, certainly this is a faith-building miracle. Interestingly enough, the flesh is cardiac muscle. Catholicism has had a strong devotion to the heart of Jesus, and for this phenomenon to be the heart muscle of a Middle Eastern man is certainly worth raising your eyebrow.

---

[2] *The Sclavo Notebooks in Diagnostics,* Collection #3, 1971.

Figure 8.3: Miraculo eucharisto

Figure 8.4: David Keys

The Eucharistic Miracle of Buenos Aires in 1996

As mentioned, some people feel that miracles no longer occur in this modern day and age. That attitude seems to imply that miracles, which were professed in the good old days, should be stated with a wink of the eye—sort of like describing a "miracle" of Santa Claus coming down a chimney. As seen in the account of the miracle at Lanciano, miracles did happen, and evidence sometimes does remain for modern man to examine. But what about modern times? Unexplainable phenomenon does happen in the modern day also. Consider the following:

On May 1, 1992, a couple of hosts were discovered on the corporals (the linen cloth on which the Eucharistic elements are placed) near the tabernacle of Santa Maria y Caballito Almagro Church in Buenos Aires, Argentina. How the hosts got there is unclear. As was the protocol for such events, the hosts were placed into a gold container of water, in order for the hosts to dissolve, and placed in the tabernacle, where other consecrated hosts also were stored to be used for future Communions. After one week's time, the container with the hosts were reexamined to see if they had dissolved. To the priest's surprise, the hosts had not dissolved and had begun to bleed. The blood was determined to be human blood. The hosts were placed into storage.

In 1996, a second event occurred. On August 15, 1996, the Solemnity of the Assumption, when Communion during the Mass was over, a woman approached the pastor and told him that she had found something at the back of the church that apparently was desecrated hosts. The priest picked them up and likewise put these in a glass of water to dissolve them. Instead of dissolving, however, the host turned into a bloody piece of meat.

Realizing the importance of these events and under the direction of the Auxiliary Bishop Jorge Bergoglio (the future Pope Francis), pictures were taken and sent to Rome; the samples were protected and stored. In 1999, it was observed that the samples had not decayed. Auxiliary Bishop Bergoglio began a further investigation. A forensic examiner determined that the tissue was cardiac tissue of a living man. At this point a German-trained neuropsychopharmacology physiologist, Castañon Ricardo Gomez from Bolivia, was commissioned to carry out additional investigations. Samples of the tissue were sent in a blind study to forensic specialists in San Francisco and to the University of Sydney in Australia. The results returned indicated that the blood was human blood, the DNA was human, and the blood cells were intact. The blood type was AB+, and the blood came from a Middle Eastern man. The tissue was heart tissue and was inflamed, showing evidence of trauma. Moreover, the tissue was still alive.

In 2005, the tissue samples were further tested. This time they were sent to Frederic Zugibe, MD, a noted forensic medical examiner at Columbia University in New York. Again, the samples were sent as part of a blind study. The specialist did not know the source of the tissue. Zugibe determined that the tissue was heart tissue, originating near the left ventricle near the aortic valve; the tissue was still alive; and the presence of white blood cells indicated trauma to the heart. Stunned to hear the source of the tissue, Zugibe compared the tissue to the pathology data taken from the heart muscle from the Lanciano miracle, which of course had occurred 1,300 years earlier. He concluded that the heart muscle belonged to the same person; that it was type AB+ blood; and that the man came from the Middle East. Moreover, Zugibe also found that the sample had the same blood characteristics as those found on the Shroud of Turin (the supposed burial cloth of a crucified man from Jerusalem in the first century), and the Sudarium of Oviedo (the suggested cloth that covered the head of an individual buried in Jerusalem in the first century). While I can't definitely state that the shroud and the sudarium belong to the same person as the heart muscle and that the person involved is Jesus of Nazareth, just look at the "coincidences" we do have—certainly interesting, miraculous coincidences: the samples are from the same man—a man from the Middle East—from the same region of the heart, and with the same blood type.[3]

The real question becomes, how much evidence does it take for one to believe? Remember when I wondered how much evidence I needed to decide I really was in Australia? Eventually, there gets to be a point where we can only say, there is no other reasonable possibility. Are God and His miracles the best explanation for this the evidence? The sciences can never conclude there is no God, because there is always a point at which God is the only answer. Consider the big bang theory for the origin of the universe. There is no answer as to where all that energy came from. Time and the universe definitely had a beginning. Even if we find that the universe arose as a "droplet" from another universe, there must always be some ultimate cause of everything, and there is only one answer that consistently applies: God.

Documentation of Additional Eucharistic Miracles

I have written about only two cases of Eucharistic miracles, but there are many more. Around 2006, the Vatican International Exhibition of the Eucharistic Miracles of the World began touring the world. In

---

[3] Most experts have come to believe that the shroud in 1988 was incorrectly carbon-dated to be from the late 1200s. That dating is no longer considered valid as, among other reasons, the area tested was involved in a fire, was partially repaired in the sixteenth century, and was contaminated with newer fibers, due to the repair. For greater detail, see Mark Antonacci's *The Resurrection of the Shroud* (New York: M. Evans and Company, Inc., 2000).

this exhibit, documents and photos of 126 Eucharistic miracles were displayed. Besides the 126 miracles reported, there are an additional thirty to forty more church-approved Eucharistic miracles, but none of those had enough information associated with them to make it into this photographic Eucharistic miracles exhibition. The exhibition's miracles are from Austria, Belgium, Caribbean Island of Martinique, Colombia, Croatia, Denmark, Egypt, France, Germany, India, Island of the Réunion (French Colony), Italy, Netherlands, Mexico, Peru, Poland, Portugal, Spain, and Switzerland. The most recent miracle included in this exhibition occurred in Chirattakonam, India, in 2001. At the time of the exhibition, though recognized by the church in Buenos Aires, the Eucharistic miracle of Buenos Aires was not formerly recognized—Vatican approval is a lengthy process. It is currently still under review as of 2014.

A Few Caveats Concerning Miracles and Faith

In discussing Eucharist miracles, the following caveats should always be considered:[4]

- Our faith is not founded on Eucharistic miracles.
- A Christian is not obliged to believe in Eucharistic miracles.
- In principle, the believer must not exclude the possibility that God may intervene in an extraordinary way in any

---

[4] The Institute of St. Clement I, Pope and Martyr, *The Eucharistic Miracles of the World* (Bardstown, KY: Eternal Life, 2009), xiii.

given moment, place, event, or person.

- The prudence of the church is fully justified, as one can run into the following risks:
- thinking God forgot something in the institution of the Eucharist
- making Sunday Eucharist secondary
- attributing excessive importance to the miraculous
- easily and excessively believing suggestions and illusions

So, let's see how the church and its people have responded to their belief that the Eucharist is the body, blood, soul, and divinity of God.

End of Chapter 8

Questions for Discussion

1. Maybe you can help me out here. The Eucharistic miracle at Lanciano has been around for 1300 years (impossible) and has been studied scientifically as to what the nature of the muscle and the blood are. The artifact of the muscle is somehow attached to the rim of bread (impossible). How can anyone deny this miracle? Certainly, no one can duplicate it.

2. There is a Vatican-approved exhibit that presents to the faithful over 200 Eucharistic miracles. True, many have no

physical evidence left behind, but many do? Is it likely that all are liars?

Chapter 9

Just Live It!

Catholic Practices Surrounding the Eucharist

A belief without a response as seen in one's daily life is not much of a belief. This is, of course, true of the belief in the Real Presence. Remembering that Catholicism was the only significant Christian church existing for the first thousand years after Christ, in practice, the question becomes, did the Catholic hierarchy and the Catholic faithful really believe in the Real Presence from the beginning of Christianity? How would we know? Written statements that the Eucharist is "the very body which hung on the tree of Calvary" or that the Eucharist is "the flesh born of Mary" could be, perhaps, just flowery words. Was it literally believed? Of course, the fact that no one is writing against those statements must give the statements as written some credence. Still, there could have been a conspiracy to destroy all the negative comments, but somehow, it would seem, at least some documents might have persevered. However, aside from the direct written word, there are a multitude of ways to know what people really believed. We should always remember that Jesus revealed God's plan through His words (not only just by His words while He walked the streets of Palestine but also including the words of Old Testament scripture) and by His deeds. James tells us, "So faith by itself, if it has no works, is dead" (James 2:17). Words are important, but if you really want to know what people believed, look at their deeds. Actions speak loudly. Action, like words, convey meaning.

So, are there certain actions that Christians have done that bespeak their belief in the Real Presence? The answer is, yes, *plenty*. And what actions would indicate that? Any action that treats the Eucharist as God would certainly indicate that one believed the Eucharist is God. The following is a partial list.

If the Eucharist is God:

- One would see the Eucharist as having infinite value; one would protect it, even be willing to die for it.
- One would not allow someone to desecrate it; therefore, one would restrict the Eucharist to those who knew what treasure they had.
- Conversely, one would want to partake of the Eucharist as often as possible, providing one was in the proper disposition, as worthy as a man could possibly be to receive God.
- One would establish liturgies centered around the Eucharist.

If it is God, one should adore it!

Is there evidence of any such activities? Luke tells us in Acts of the apostles that the early believers devoted themselves "to the apostles' teaching and fellowship, to the breaking of bread and the prayers"

(Acts 2:42). Thus, the "breaking of the bread" was important and associated with "the" prayers, not just any prayers. This sounds like a kind of liturgy, but was it?

The Eucharist in the Early Church

Let's skip a hundred years from the Paschal event and the institution of the Eucharist to the writings of St. Justin Martyr from around AD 150–160, as found in chapters 66 and 67 of his First Apology.[1] St. Justin Martyr was a second-century apologist for the church who wrote the Emperor Antonius Pius (AD 138–162) with a description of Christian beliefs in an attempt to stop the persecution of the fledgling church.[2] His writings give a window into the early church.

Chapter 6. Of the Eucharist

> "And this food is called among us Εὐχαριστία [the Eucharist], of which *no one is allowed to partake but the man who believes* that the things which we teach are true, and who has been *washed with the washing* that is for the remission of sins, and unto regeneration, and

---

[1] Translated by Marcus Dods and George Reith. From Ante-Nicene Fathers, vol. 1. Edited by Alexander Roberts, James Donaldson, and A. Cleveland Coxe (Buffalo, NY: Christian Literature Publishing Co., 1885). Revised and edited for New Advent by Kevin Knight. http://www.newadvent.org/fathers/0126.htm.

[2] http://en.wikipedia.org/wiki/Justin_Martyr.

who is so living as Christ has enjoined. For not as
common bread and common drink do we receive these;
but in like manner as Jesus Christ our Saviour, having
been made flesh by the Word of God, had both flesh and
blood for our salvation …"[3] (italics added).

Note that already in the second century, the practice was to
allow only those who believed that the Eucharist was the body and
blood of Jesus (for that was what was taught) to receive the
Eucharist. Visitors who were not Catholics (a term already used by
Ignatius of Antioch years before) could not receive Communion.
This was—and is—to protect the Eucharist, because it is much
more than bread and wine; it is the body and blood of Jesus.

In addition, those who receive the Eucharist must not only be
baptized into the faith but also be living a moral life "as Christ has
enjoined." Those in the state of sin cannot receive the Eucharist.
These teachings still exist.

In chapter 6, we also see that the Eucharist is associated with
specific prayers. The Eucharist, then, is given to the faithful as part
of a liturgy.

"so likewise have we been taught that the food which is
blessed by the prayer of His word, and from which our

[3] Translated by Marcus Dods and George Reith. From Ante-Nicene
Fathers, vol. 1. Edited by Alexander Roberts, James Donaldson, and A.
Cleveland Coxe (Buffalo, NY: Christian Literature Publishing Co.,
1885). Revised and edited for New Advent by Kevin Knight.
http://www.newadvent.org/fathers/0126.htm.

blood and flesh by transmutation are nourished, is the flesh and blood of that Jesus who was made flesh" [4] (italics added).

Chapter 6. Weekly Worship of the Christians

"On the day called Sunday, all who live in cities or in the country gather together to one place, and the memoirs of the apostles or the writings of the prophets are read, as long as time permits; then, when the reader has ceased, the president verbally instructs, and exhorts to the imitation of these good things." [5]

This liturgy that surrounds the Eucharist was apparently an important event and was attended on Sunday by all who lived close by. Today is no different. We recognize the Mass as a source of grace and an opportunity to worship God in community. Part of the service was to read from the Gospels and then to listen to the priest (the presider), who gave a homily on the Gospel reading. Sounds familiar. Catholics now call this the Liturgy of the Word.

"Then we all rise together and pray, and, as we before said, when our prayer is ended, bread and wine and water are brought, and the president in like manner offers prayers and thanksgivings, according to his ability, …" [6]

---

[4] Ibid.

[5] Ibid.

[6] Ibid.

This references the procession of the gifts and associated prayers, which is part of our offertory. Then the priest, being given the "ability" by virtue of his ordination, consecrates the Eucharist, saying the Eucharistic prayers.

> "and the people assent, saying Amen;"

This refers to the Great Amen, which is still part of the Mass ("through Him, with Him, in Him ... Amen!"). The following addresses the actual distribution and partaking of Communion.

> "and there is a distribution to each, and a participation of that over which thanks have been given,"[7]

Communion is given to the faithful.

> "and to those who are absent a portion is sent by the deacons."[8]

Note that this confirms that the bread once consecrated remains consecrated. Also, observe that only authorized persons—in this case, the deacons—could distribute the Eucharist. There exists other evidence that nonordained ministers could deliver the Eucharist, and that the laity could take the Eucharist home, particularly during times of persecution. These special

---

[7] Ibid.

[8] Ibid.

circumstances also brought about special concerns—that of abuse or neglect. Tertullian, among others, warned that anyone who possessed the Eucharist must be concerned that even one crumb or drop might fall to the ground. [9]

Continuing with Justin Martyr's writing:

> "And they who are well to do, and willing, give what each thinks fit; and what is collected is deposited with the president, who succours the orphans and widows and those who, through sickness or any other cause, are in want, and those who are in bonds and the strangers sojourning among us, and in a word takes care of all who are in need."

As in the current Sunday Mass, a collection is taken up for the poor and presented to the priest. From the writings of Justin Martyr, we see that, indeed, the church considered the Eucharist to be a most precious gift from God.

Who can be the presider?

St. Justin Martyr specifically mentions the President as the "presider" over the Mass. Just whom is this referring to? Can anyone say the prayers, do the motions, etc. and say the Mass, including consecrating the Bread and Wine? For this, let's go back even earlier in time and, again, look at the writings of Ignatius of Antioch.

---

[9] http://www.newadvent.org/cathen/14520c.htm

In his letter to the Smyrnaeans, Ignatius states:

> "*You must all follow THE BISHOP* as Jesus Christ follows
> the Father, and *the presbyters* as you would the Apostles.
> Reverence *the deacons* as you would the command of God.
> Let no one do anything of concern to the church without
> *THE BISHOP*. Let that be considered a valid Eucharist
> **which is celebrated by *THE BISHOP*, or by *one whom he***
> ***appoints.***

And whom did the Bishop appoint for this task if he were not consecrating the Eucharist? None other than the presbyters. From the
beginning it was bishops, priests, and deacons. Bishops, priests,
and deacons were all ordained by the laying on of hands by a
Bishop who succeeded from the first Apostles. The bishops were
true overseers and especially had the God-given authority to con-
secrate the Eucharist and to forgive or retain sins, acting in the
Person of Christ (*Persona Christi*). This ability they shared with
the presbyters, but not the deacons, whose role was primarily to
serve and to preach.

Is this in the New Testament? Yes! In the New Testament,
Episkopos—the word for bishop (or a variant), is found six times
(1 Tim 3:1, 3:2, Titus 1:7, 1 Pet 2:25, Acts 1:20, and Phil 1:1). In
Acts, Judas's office (bishopric in KJV) must be filled. Timothy and
Titus are particularly show the succession of bishops. *Presbyteros*
(or its variant)—is all over the place. As you probably know, most
Protestant bibles translate the Greek word "*presbyteros*" into Eng-
lish as Elders. Truly, most were probably older. However, if you

look up the etymology of the word "priest," you will discover that "priest" is derived from the Greek word "*presbyteros*" and is not the same as the Greek word the Jews use for High Priest (*archi-eréas*) or Levitical priest (*hierous*). The Catholic priest is different from a Jewish priest. *Diakonos (or its variant)*—the word for deacon is used many times. The most famous use of diakonos is in Acts 6 when Peter selects and ordains seven Hellenist men to serve the tables. The most famous of those deacons were and are St. Stephen and St. Philip.

Additional Evidence That the Eucharist Was Considered Holy

What are other signs that the Eucharist is holy? The early church believed in the reservation of the Eucharist; that is, they believed that the Eucharist remained the body and blood of Jesus Christ, even after the liturgy had concluded. Because the Eucharist remained the body and blood of Jesus and thus would be holy, they stored the Eucharist in tabernacles. This is seen in the late fourth century. After Constantine stopped the persecutions of the Christians, and Christianity could become openly visible without fear of reprisal, the consecrated hosts were sometimes stored in ornamental metal doves that hung above the altar. The Eucharist was stored in a precious metal container because it contained the most precious thing there could be.

Figure 9.1: Dove Tabernacle

Others signs of such belief in the reservation of the Eucharist are seen in such acts as the rite of *fermentum*. The rite of *fermentum* is the transferring of a piece of the consecrated Eucharistic bread, sometimes dipped in the consecrated wine, from one bishop to another as a sign of mutual unity. This practice goes back to AD 120.[10] In addition, as seen in the writings of Justin Martyr, noted above, the Eucharist could be taken to the sick or even kept for future use, such as done by hermits. Another practice that shows the belief in the reservation of the Eucharist is the practice of wearing a "perula" around the neck. The perula was similar to a small pouch that contained the Eucharist.[11]

But if the Eucharist is truly the body and blood of Jesus, one should do more than just carry it around. One should adore it, because it is Jesus. The word is adore, not venerate, such as one might do for the relic of a saint or even the saint himself/herself.

---

[10] http://www.therealpresence.org/eucharst/pea/history.htm.

[11] http:// www.therealpresence.org/eucharst/pea/history.htm.

Adoration is reserved for God alone. Indeed, the early church did adore the Eucharist. St. Augustine directly stated this. He is quoted as saying, "It is a sin not to adore the Eucharist." [12] As early as the fifth century, in some dioceses, newly baptized Christians practiced perpetual adoration (that is, 24/7) and adored the Eucharist for the first eight days after becoming Catholic. [13] In addition, in another display of belief, Eucharistic processions were piously "paraded" down public streets, with the consecrated host

Figure 9.2: A typical sunburst pattern

exposed in a monstrance (see figure 9.2). These processions began shortly after the Berengarius heresy in the eleventh century.

With the initiation of the Feast of Corpus Christi in 1264, together with the composing of appropriate hymns by St. Thomas Aquinas, as commissioned by Pope Urban IV, benediction (a special form of Eucharistic adoration, accompanied by specific liturgical prayers and the raising of the host in a monstrance by a

---

[12] James O'Connor, *The Hidden Manna*, 2nd ed. (San Francisco: Ignatius Press, 2005), 58.

[13] http://www.therealpresence.org/eucharst/pea/history.htm.

priest or deacon before all the people) became popular. Not surprisingly, the feast of Corpus Christi and the benediction liturgy of St. Thomas Aquinas began subsequent to the occurrence of a nearby Eucharistic miracle at Bolsena-Orvieto, Italy.[14] (Note: Orvieto is near Rome. Pope Urban IV was residing there at the time of the miracle in 1263.)

Other protection of sacredness of the Eucharist involved restricting the age of persons receiving the Eucharist. In the early centuries of Christianity, infants were allowed to receive the Eucharist, and, in fact, this practice continues today in the Eastern rites of the Catholic Church and in Orthodox churches.[15] However, this was changed for the Western Latin rite in 813 at the Council of Tours, when the age of first reception was moved back to "age of discretion," which many took to be twelve to fourteen years of age. Now the age of first reception of the Eucharist is generally taken, but not mandated, to occur around seven years of age. The net result of delaying the reception of communion to a later date is that the initial reception of Communion became a rite of passage in a Roman Catholic child's life, and it was only a matter of time before First Communion celebrations began to occur, a practice that continues today. A particular example of the significance of First Communion is seen in the oft-reported story

---

[14] Joan Cruz, *Eucharistic Miracles* (Rockford, IL: Tan Books and Publishers, 1987), 59.

[15] Patrick Morrisroe, "Communion of Children," *The Catholic Encyclopedia*, vol. 4 (New York: Robert Appleton Company, 1908). Accessed 30 Oct. 2013, http://www.newadvent.org/cathen/04170b.htm.

that Napoleon, who was no great friend of the church, purportedly said that the day of his First Communion was the happiest day of his life.[16] From personal experience, the significance continues, and every Catholic with whom I am acquainted remembers his or her First Communion.

One last consideration (although I am sure there are many other examples)—let's look at the preparation for receiving the Eucharist. The preparation should be mental, spiritual, and physical, reflecting the fact that, after all, we are both body and soul. The reading of scripture and the saying of prayers before Mass is one way to prepare mentally and spiritually before reception. Perhaps this approach is not as common as it should be, but the reading of scripture certainly is contained within Mass. To further focus our minds on the upcoming Communion, fasting is employed. This has a long history in the church. Pope Pius XII, in his encyclical *Dominus Christus* in 1953, stated:

> From the very earliest time the custom was observed of administering the Eucharist to the faithful who were fasting. Toward the end of the fourth century fasting was prescribed by many Councils for those who were going to celebrate the Eucharistic Sacrifice. So it was that the Council of Hippo in the year 393 issued this decree: 'The Sacrament of the altar shall be offered only by those who are fasting.' Shortly afterward, in the year 397, the Third Council of Carthage issued this same

---

[16] Renee Casin, "*Napoleon and Religion*," http://www.napoleonicsociety.com/english/religcasina.htm.

command, using the very same words. At the beginning of the fifth century, this custom can be called quite common and immemorial. Hence St. Augustine affirms that the Holy Eucharist is always received by people who are fasting and likewise that this custom is observed throughout the entire world. [17]

In addition, the choice of fasting as a means of preparation should not be surprising, as we have a Jewish background, or as Pope Pius XI expressed it in 1938, "Spiritually we [Catholics] are Semites." [18] In chapter 2, we saw that the Aaronic high priests fasted (and abstained from sexual activities) prior to consuming the Bread of the Presence that was offered in the temple. Fasting remains a powerful way for us to focus our attention, because we must actively remind ourselves not to eat or drink, while at the same time our bodies remind us of our need for sustenance. By not giving in, we profess our belief that the Eucharist is far superior to any earthly sustenance that we may receive.

Many Catholic practices in our present and past history show the common thread of respect, reverence, and adoration for the Eucharist, as befitting what the Eucharist is—the very body, blood, soul, and divinity of our Lord Jesus Christ. Let's now see how God has responded to our faith.

---

[17] Pius XII, *Christus Dominus*, http://www.papalencyclicals.net/Pius12/P12CHDOM.HTM.

[18] *La Documentation Catholique* (1938), 1459–1460; cited in Johannes G. M. Willebrands, *Church and Jewish People: New Considerations* (Paulist, 1992), 60.

End of Chapter 9

Questions for Discussion

1. What do you remember of your first Holy Communion?

2. What do you remember of your last Holy Communion?

Chapter 10

God's Wonderful Response

The Healing Miracles of the Eucharist

God is so good to us. He created the whole universe, not for His benefit but for ours. He provided a world for us to live that is filled with great natural beauty, such as mountains, oceans, flowers, autumn colors, and on and on. He populated it with plants and animals to provide us with food, clothing, shelter, and even, to some extent, companionship. He created man and gave him the greatest gift when He gave man a free will—the ability to love. When man chose himself over God and sinned, God promised to make it right. He even sent His Son to die a most wretched death on a cross, so that we might again have communion with Him. Yet we all have, at one time or another, turned our backs on Him. Still, He pursues us, waiting for us to choose Him. To help us love Him, He established His church to provide for us special graces through the sacraments, through its teachings, and through His Word, as recorded and interpreted by the church. Yet He still does more. He has given us Eucharistic miracles to "help our unbelief." And when we are in need and seek Him in faith (or sometimes through the faith of others), He responds, if it is in our interests, with miracles in our lives.

Of particular interest for this book are miracles directly

involving the Eucharist. We have previously discussed in chapter 8 the doctrinal Eucharistic miracles, which confirm that the Eucharist is truly the flesh and blood of Jesus. In a way, the Eucharistic miracles are teaching miracles that are designed to increase our faith. However, there are many other miracles associated with the Eucharist that are of a different nature. These are miracles of great mercy and typically involve a healing. They are miracles of faith. Often, the miracles are brought about not by our own faith, but by someone else's belief in the Real Presence. There should be no surprise here. During Jesus's earthly life, He performed many miracles, and many of His miracles were based on the request of others (e.g., Peter's mother-in-law, the centurion's servant, the raising of Lazarus). And if the Eucharist is truly Christ, how can we be surprised when a miracle occurs in which the Eucharist is the very source of the miracle? Indeed, when God chooses to heal through the Eucharist, whether He is responding due to our faith or that of another, God often chooses to act in a total surprise to us.

Example: Healing Miracles of the Eucharist

The criteria used to denote a miracle

The following examples in which the Eucharist played a major role in a dramatic miracle of healing all occurred in Lourdes, France, which is located in the foothills of the Pyrenees Mountains. These miracles were chosen not only because they involve the Eucharist but also because of the strict guidelines and investigation required for an event at Lourdes to be called a miracle. Lourdes is no ordinary place. Miracles began to occur in 1858 after the Blessed Virgin Mary appeared to Bernadette Soubirous. A spring appeared at the site of the appearance, and those who bathed in the spring began experiencing miraculous healings. Often, the Eucharist has also served as a cause of the healings. All healings were meticulously investigated and documented, and that continues today. Part of the process to be an official miracle at Lourdes involves the inspection of those healed by a team of doctors and then a follow-up each year for three years, in order to demonstrate that the miracle was permanent. The following are some of the additional criteria for a Lourdes miracle:

- The miracle must be instantaneous. Healings must occur on the spot.
- The patient's condition must be well documented, both beforehand and afterward.
- Annual follow-ups must be maintained.
- The condition must have been serious—sore shoulders and minor arthritis would not count.

The Story of John Traynor[1]

John Traynor (1883–1943) was a World War I veteran. On

---

[1] This story was condensed from Paul Glynn's *Healing Fire of Christ* (San Francisco: Ignatius Press, 2003), 69–74.

October 8, 1914, at the Battle of Dunkirk, he was wounded in the head by a piece of shrapnel. It took five weeks after removal of the metal from his brain before he recovered consciousness. Recovering from that injury, he was soon sent to the Suez Canal, where he took a bullet to his right knee. It was a clean wound, and he soon rejoined his company. He was sent to the Gallipoli Peninsula, in what is now modern Turkey. There, once again, he was injured. This time, during a bayonet charge toward the Turkish trenches on May 8, 1915, he was hit by three bullets; two bullets went through the right side of his chest and passed through cleanly, but a third bullet severed the nerves in the brachial plexus and in the right axilla. This damage numbed the skin, paralyzed his right arm, and eventually resulted in atrophy of the arm. Multiple surgeries to repair the damage were unsuccessful. To make matters worse, Traynor began to suffer epileptic seizures while on the ship that returned him to England. Once home in England, additional surgery was performed but to no avail. Finally, it was recommended that his arm be amputated, but Traynor refused. He was discharged and given a military pension.

In 1919, Traynor spent ten months in a special treatment center for epileptics. Eventually, he received additional brain surgery, which not only was unsuccessful but left a one-inch diameter opening on the right side of his skull, from which one could see the brain pulsing under the skin! Sometimes when he coughed, there was even a protrusion of dura matter outside the hole. With memory loss, headaches, right arm paralysis, and the inability to walk, it is evident that Traynor was, as it is sometimes called, a medical train wreck.

What to do? A friend, a Mrs. Cunningham, mentioned that the parish priest was taking a group to Lourdes, France, the site of great healings. There, those needing healing would enter into baths fed by a spring that originated during the apparitions to Bernadette Soubirous by the Blessed Virgin Mother. Even though he knew that not everyone received a physical healing, Traynor decided to go anyway and was somewhat surprised when the parish priest and others tried to discourage him—they feared that the trip would literally kill Traynor. Because of the controversy and the fact that Traynor was a veteran of WWI, the local Liverpool newspaper ran a series of human-interest stories about him. Eventually, Traynor's will won out, and amid a huge gathering at the train station, he departed on July 21, 1923, for his journey to Lourdes.

Traynor did nearly die on the journey, but after arriving at Lourdes, he proceeded through the process and was bathed naked in the 53-degrees-Fahrenheit water in the *piscines* (French for pool)—all seemingly to no avail but not to his detriment. In the second of the nine baths typically received, he suffered an epileptic seizure, and blood even flowed from his mouth. As it turned out, however, that was to be his last seizure. After the

Figure 10.1: John Traynor heading to Lourdes

ninth bath, he felt a change and kicked and thrashed about. Subsequently, he was taken to the square in front of the Rosary Church, where a Eucharistic procession and a blessing of the sick with the Eucharist was about to take place. The Archbishop of Rheims, carrying the monstrance, passed in front of Traynor. He stopped before Traynor, made the sign of the cross with the monstrance, and then moved on. Suddenly, Traynor's paralyzed arm became agitated. He burst his

Figure 10.2: John Traynor serving as a *brancardier*

bandages as he made the sign of the cross with the formerly paralyzed arm. He tried to rise, but the attendants, fearing another epileptic fit, gave him a shot to knock him out and returned Traynor to the Asile hospital, where he was staying. The next morning, he got out of bed onto his knees to say a rosary and then ran barefoot to the grotto and prayed. Then he returned to the hospital. Needless to say, all were shocked.

As required by those at Lourdes, he underwent a series of tests for documentation purposes. The doctors who examined him recorded the following:

- He can walk perfectly.
- He has recovered full use of his arm.
- He has recovered sensation in his legs.
- The opening in his skull has diminished considerably. [Eventually, it became obliterated, leaving only a small indentation.]

Returning to Liverpool, he was once again greeted by huge crowds. John Traynor was so grateful for his miracle that he not only returned for annual inspections but even served for many years as a volunteer *brancardier* (one who helps the sick enter the *piscines*). He remained strong and even could be seen in his sixties carrying a two-hundred-pound bag of coal on his shoulders. His miracle was complete. His miracle was permanent.

He eventually died of a strangulated hernia, probably due to the coal bags he carried and unrelated to his prior military injuries.

Brother Leo Schwager[2]

Lourdes is not the only place where Eucharistic healings take place, of course, but their documentation is so strong that the data cannot be rationally dismissed. Something definitely goes on there. Another such case is Brother Leo Schwager, a Swiss Benedictine monk, who arrived in Lourdes in April 1952 at the age

---

[2] Ibid.

of twenty-eight.

At the time of his arrival at Lourdes, Brother Leo was bed-ridden, paralyzed, permanently catheterized, weighed less than 103 pounds, and was barely conscious. He had been suffering from a number of ailments since 1946 and in 1950 had been diagnosed with advanced multiple sclerosis. On the morning of April 30, he was taken to the baths at Lourdes, with no beneficial effects. That afternoon he was returned to the baths, again

Figure 10.3: A young, healthy Brother Leo Schwager

with no effects. Feeling weak and in pain, he desired only to return to his room, but instead, he was taken to the Rosary Church Esplanade for the blessing of the sick. As in the case of John Traynor, the bishop, who was processing with the monstrance, gave him the blessing of the sick. Suddenly, it was as if an electric shock jolted his body. He became unconscious, and upon awakening, he found himself on his knees in front of the monstrance. All his pain had vanished. Dr. Jeger, who had accompanied the group, rushed up to see what happened. Brother Leo simply said, "I'm well, I'm healthy!" He thanked God and began praying the *Magnificat* (the song of Mary after her visitation to Elizabeth, as told in Luke 1:46–55). He walked back to the *Accueil Notre Dame* (Reception Center

Figure 10.4: Brother Leo Schwager in 1996

of Our Lady), where he was staying, and was examined by a number of doctors who had accompanied the Swiss group to Lourdes. Ordered to stay in his bedroom, he spent a sleepless night, praying and giving thanks. The next morning, despite recommendations of the doctors, the famished Benedictine monk ate a large breakfast and later was examined by eighteen doctors and was questioned for four hours. Perhaps the highlight of his testimony was Brother Leo's insistence that he was thrown out of the wheelchair onto his knees before the Eucharist. In spite of these dramatic circumstances, the Lourdes Medical Bureau took six and a half years before they accepted his case for investigation. (It takes a lot to impress the Bureau!) During that interim time, Brother Leo's cure was simply referred to as "medically inexplicable," joining 2,500 other such cases that had arisen since 1883. In 1960, the Lourdes Medical Bureau ruled the case as a true cure. At that point, Brother Leo's bishop, Fribourg-Lausanne, initiated a canonical investigation. Eventually, on December 18, 1960, Brother Leo's cure was declared a miracle by the canonical commission. As of 1996, Brother Leo still showed no signs of his former disease.

Jeanne Fretel

Born in 1914 in Sougeal, France, Jeanne led a simple life.

Being poor, she entered the workforce at a young age at the local hospital in nearby Rennes. By 1938, at the age of twenty-four, Jeanne began to have severe abdominal pains. Eventually, she was diagnosed with tubercular peritonitis, a particularly dreadful disease that caused pain and swelling in the abdomen. Fortunately, despite the fact that she had limited financial means, she was able to receive quality medical care, due to her employment at the hospital and due to the kindness of the physicians. In 1939, surgery was performed to remove a tuberculous cyst on an ovary. Later that year, a laparoscopy was performed, in which a special instrument is inserted into the abdomen to view the contents of the abdomen. Later, a disastrous second laparoscopy was performed, which led to a stercoral fistula and the seepage of feces out of the intestine. After three years and four surgeries, the fistula was repaired, but the tuberculous bacteria had gone to her back, and her stomach became rock hard.

On October 4, 1948—tired and exhausted, weighing less than ninety-seven pounds, receiving three or four shots of morphine a day for her pain, with large holes in

Figure 10.5: A young, healthy Jeanne Fretel

her tuberculous-infected jawbones—she accompanied a group to Lourdes. By the time she reached Lourdes on October 5, she was unconscious and was hand-carried to the *piscines* at Lourdes. On the fourth day, she was taken, still unconscious, to the Mass of the Sick. The priest administering the Communion, noting her poor condition, had decided to pass by her but was then convinced by one of Jeanne's stretcher-bearers to put a tiny piece of the consecrated host into Jeanne's mouth. Instantly, she woke up, alert, and asked where she was. They then took her to the baths, where she felt a presence sitting her up and placing her hands on her stomach. However, no one was there. At that point, she knew that her stomach had been healed. The swelling and pain had disappeared. Taken back to the hospital, she saw her doctor, who confirmed that the swelling had disappeared. Desiring to eat, she later stated, "I enjoyed the kind of meal I had not eaten for ten years!"—a phenomenon noted in many Lourdes cures. She got up from the table and then walked back to the *piscines* on her own (she hadn't walked for three years), where she took a shower while standing, with no fatigue. The next day, she met with other doctors from the Lourdes Medical Bureau and demonstrated her miraculous newfound health to them.

Returning to her hospital in Rennes, she met with her local doctor, a declared agnostic who was "hostile to religion," who had assumed she must have died by this time. Seeing Jeanne enter the room, the doctor left the room crying, so great was his shock. Over the years, Jeanne continued to work at the hospital and to return annually to Lourdes, where she was seen helping other pilgrims, fifty years after her miraculous cure.

Figure 10.6: Jeanne Fretel, years after her miraculous recovery

These three cases are but a drop in the bucket of the healing miracles of the Eucharist. They were chosen because they were so well investigated and documented, but there are many other events. Perhaps the most powerful indicator of the truth of these events lies in the conversion of those outside the faith who actually knew the individual. The biggest truth, however, is the great love God has for His people and His continued desire to use miraculous signs, just as Jesus did during His time on earth. God remains a personal, involved God. He not only loves us, but He wishes for us to believe that in the Eucharist, the bread and wine really do become the body and blood of Jesus Christ.

As Jesus Himself said, "Do you not believe that I am in the Father and the Father in me? The words that I say to you I do not speak on my own authority; but the Father who dwells in me does his works. Believe me that I am in the Father and the Father in me; or else believe me *for the sake of the works themselves*" (John 14:10–11, italics added). If we have difficulty believing in the Real Presence because the artifacts of bread and wine that remain get in the way, we should believe because of the great works that have occurred in the healing miracles of the Eucharist.

End of Chapter 10

Questions for Discussion

1. Many people are skeptical of healing miracles. True, there are cases in which psychological issues may result in thinking one has had a miraculous healing; however, some are so well documented, as in the examples of Chapter 10. How can one convince the eternal skeptic?

2. I have been told many times by physicians that the study of the body, and incidents in the care of their patients have convinced them that there must be a supreme being far greater than us. Have you ever asked your physician if they have ever witnessed such an apparently incredible event?

Chapter 11

It's No End, Just the Beginning

I started this book by acknowledging that the concept of the host and wine becoming the body and blood really is not a rational thought, according to our senses. However, the question of interest is not whether we believe it is rational but instead, whether it is true. I pointed out that even some areas of science, such as quantum theory, have theorems that may be considered "absurd" yet are true. I pointed out that we come to know something only because we accept the evidence presented by those we believe and trust. With enough evidence, we can eventually get to the point of saying, "I believe it is true!" Thus, when I went to Australia, I could quickly come to believe that I was really there, because I trusted that the street guides, the signs along the road, the language spoken, and the customs agents were really trustworthy and not part of a hoax. I believed, because I had a "preponderance of evidence" from trustworthy sources to convince me.

I hope I likewise have presented a "preponderance of evidence" for you in regard to the Eucharist. I have shown Old Testament typology of the Eucharist; Jesus's very promise that He would give us His flesh; the institution of that promise; the actions and words of the church, from the beginning of the church and throughout the years, indicating Jesus's words were literal; miracles from God, showing us that the Eucharist is true flesh and blood; and finally, miracles of healing associated with the reception or presence of the Eucharist. But don't just take my word on this evidence. Investigate the facts yourself. Many nonbelievers have come to believe in the Real Presence simply because the "preponderance of evidence"—the consistency with scripture, the historical teachings and actions of the church, and the phenomenology associated with "events" surrounding the Eucharist. Reread the book, this time having the whole picture in mind. Remember the advice of St. Augustine from chapter 1: "Seek not to understand so you may believe, but believe so you may understand."[1] There will always be mystery. Just because one does not fully understand the mystery does not mean it is not true.

Does It Matter?

After all this discussion, does it make a difference whether or not one believes in the Real Presence? The answer is yes for a number of reasons.

- Jesus promised He would send the Spirit to guide His church "in all truth" (John 16:13) and that Jesus would

---

[1] *Ten Homilies on the First Epistle of John* Tractate XXIX on John 7:14–18, §6. *A Select Library of the Nicene And Post-Nicene Fathers of the Christian Church Volume VII by St. Augustine, chapter VII (1888) as translated by Philip Schaff.*

build His church "and the powers of death shall not prevail against it" (Matthew 16:18). If the early church has always viewed the Eucharist as being real, then it simply must be true. To believe otherwise is to believe that Jesus allowed incorrect doctrine to be preached by His church for century upon century. In other words, the Holy Spirit failed to guide the church in all truth, and Satan would have prevailed against the church during those years.

- Doctrine does sometimes divide congregations. Thus, many churches do not discuss doctrine often, concentrating on loving God and living a moral life. Loving God and living a moral life are certainly good things, but neglecting doctrine in order to maintain harmony means that the full gospel is not being taught. Doctrine contains revelation about God, so doctrine really is important. Without true doctrine, we could be led astray, perhaps miss out on some of God's great gifts, or fail to enter into as deep a union with God as we might otherwise. Paul warns the readers of his epistles many times about the dangers of false doctrine, as he also warned them that "any one who eats and drinks without discerning the body, eats and drinks judgment upon himself" (1 Corinthians 11:29).

- "If we, or an angel from heaven, should preach to you a gospel contrary to that which we preached to you, let him be accursed" (Galatians 1:8).

- "Guard the truth that has been entrusted to you by the Holy Spirit who dwells within us" (2 Timothy 1:14).

- "For the time is coming when people will not endure sound

teaching, but having itching ears they will accumulate for themselves teachers to suit their own likings, and will turn away from listening to the truth" (2 Timothy 2:3–4).

- Living the Christian life is difficult. We need all the graces we can receive. Those in Old Testament times did not have all the graces that we Christians have.

- Ezekiel, an Old Testament prophet, prophesized that with the coming of the Messiah, things would be different. He quoted the Lord as saying, "I will put my Spirit in you and move you to follow my decrees" (Ezekiel 36:27).

- Jesus is the source of all grace. Through the Eucharist, we receive this ultimate source of grace, because we directly receive Jesus. We should take advantage of this. Jesus tells, "He who eats my flesh and drinks my blood abides in me, and I in him. As the living Father sent me, and I live because of the Father, so he who eats me will live because of me" (John 6:56–57).

- Partake of the Eucharist as often as possible. It will help you to overcome your faults and to be more loving, and it will help you endure suffering.

Final Words

Be open to and pursue truth, changing your life as truth dictates. And pray, pray, pray for the gift of faith!

Chapter 11: Questions for Discussion

1) How has the Eucharist affected your life?

Appendix A

Discussion Questions

Chapter 1: Questions for Discussion

1. Can you name other "facts of life" which apparently make no sense, but are indeed true?

    Response: Space/Time warping due to the effects of massive bodies is apparently a real event. Space is apparently warped, like the surface of water is when you sit on a raft. That is objects gravitate "down" due to the bigger mass. Objects never gravitate away from the matter, so one always falls "down." Of course, unless Physics returns to the days of an ether medium in space, there is no surface, like a water surface to actually warp. Time also warps. Time may be a dimension and it is useful to mathematically treat time as a dimension, but really what does that mean? Yet treating space and time this way, does seem to model physical realities.

2. Have you ever experienced coincidences which later in life, no longer seem to be a coincidence, but rather part of God's plan for you?

Response: It is not unusual for a person to realize that a chance happening ended up altering one's life. I remember, one spring day when I was in graduate school, seeing a magazine with a cover page article on the use of Physics in Medicine. Just curious, I called an individual who was mentioned in the article and was working with linear accelerators at nearby Barnes hospital in St. Louis. Sure enough, that individual mentioned in an article on physics in medicine was no longer there, but his replacement answered the phone and stated they had just purchased some new equipment and were about to start a search for a young graduate student (cheap labor) to work over the summer to characterize the radiation coming out of the machine. Needless to say, I got the summer job, and soon began a 38-year career in Medical Physics. Great timing, huh?

Chapter 2: Questions for Discussion

1) Which of the Types presented in Chapter 2 is most significant for you?

   Response: There is no one answer here, but I would say the type of the Passover Lamb, serving as an image of the promised one who, not only would suffer and be put to death for us, but also whose flesh must be consumed in order for us to receive eternal life.

2) The people of Israel's very lives were saved by the nutrition provided by the manna, yet they grumbled and were not satisfied. They failed to see the daily miracle of the manna. The Eucharist is more glorious than the manna, yet many "believers" fail to see the miracle of the Eucharist. How can you maintain a hunger for the Eucharist?

Response: Eucharistic adoration is a great way to maintain the realization that the Consecrated Host one is adoring is not just a symbol but is the real thing.

Chapter 3: Questions for Discussion

1) The Multiplication of the loaves and the fishes in John 6 is a type of the Eucharist. One detail of the miracle is that Jesus has the disciples gather up the remnants not consumed (Jn 6:12). He did not just let the people dispose of the remnants anywhere, such as on the ground. How does that foreshadow the way we treat the Eucharistic hosts which are left unconsumed after a Mass?

Response: It is Catholic teaching that the remnants of a consecrated host remain the Body, Blood, Soul, and Divinity of Jesus Christ, as long as the elements remain. Certainly, some of the loaves and fishes blessed by Jesus probably was originally discarded during the dining process. Jesus has the Apostles collect all food Jesus blessed, because by that blessing (as by the waters of the Jordan river when

Jesus was baptized), the miraculous food would become holy.

2) The comments on the different translations of the Our Father in Matthew and Luke in the Vulgate show the difficulty in the translation of Scripture into any language. If the meaning of the words of Scripture depends on the translator, how can we rely on the validity of Scripture? In other words, is there an entity which has been promised to be led into all Truth who can properly interpret Scripture?

   Response: It is the Bishops of the Church who, collectively, have been promised that the Paraclete would come to and whom the Paraclete would lead to Truth.

Chapter 4: Questions for Discussion

1) Only the Apostles attended the Last Supper in which Jesus instituted the Eucharist. Jesus only told them to "Do this." He could have told those in attendance at the feeding of the five thousand (Jn 6) or at the feeding of the four thousand (Mt 15) to "Do this", but he didn't. Apparently, authority was only given to the Apostles who were the first Bishops of His Church (See Acts 1:20 "office" -> episkopen (Greek) -> Bishopric (KJV)). The term for Bishop could also have been translated Overseer. Certainly, in Church history, the Bishops have overseen their Episcopate or their Diocese. How has this particular authority—to confect the

Eucharist, been passed onto our current day Bishops? How do our current day priests get their authority?

Response: Bishops have passed on this authority to other Bishops through the laying on of hands through Apostolic Succession. Like the early day of the Church, today's presbyters receive their authority by being ordained by and given permission from a bishop who has succeeded the Apostles.

2) Many Catholics do not believe in the Real Presence. Does the host and the wine becoming the body and blood of Jesus depend on whether the person believes it happens?

Response: No, we are not in charge. We do not decide. What happens when the Host and
Wine are consecrated is independent of us. When standing in the communion line, all receive the Real Presence whether one understands that to be true or not.

Chapter 5: Questions for Discussion

1) John's gospel is believed to have been written much later than the gospels of Matthew, Mark, and Luke. If the Eucharist is so significant, why didn't John write about the institution of the Eucharist. Instead, John seems to write about everything else that happened on that last Passover night before Jesus died. Why is that?

Response: It is believed that John wrote his gospel to fill in some of the gaps and theological inferences that may not have been stated in Matthew, Mark, and Luke. John, after all, was very theological and wanted his readers to know the theological significance of what was happening in his gospel. Different witnesses describe different things. In describing a car accident, it is not unusual for the eyewitnesses to focus on their own interpretation of an accident. A physician might describe the events far differently than an individual not trained in medicine. This does not make their reports in error or make the other descriptions inadequate.

2) It has been said by some that the Eucharist is medicine for the spiritually sick. Paul said the opposite. He said that receiving the Eucharist unworthily makes one gravely ill. How can you reconcile these disparate concepts?

Response: It is still amazing that many, including myself at times in my life, knowingly received the Eucharist unworthily. However, there are degrees of sickness. Medicine can be beneficial for the physically sick, but they can't be dead already. Paul is speaking of those already spiritually dead. They are creating further damage to their souls by knowingly doing what they know is wrong. The health of one's soul can lift one up or cause greater distress to any individual.

Chapter 6: Questions for Discussion

1) In the 4th century, Arius convinced up to 80% of the bishops at that time that Jesus was not God and did not exist for all time. This was corrected over a period of time over three centuries by a number of councils beginning with the Council of Nicaea (AD 325) though the 3rd council of Constantinople (AD 680). Can you name any period in Church history, where the Church said the Eucharist was not the Body and Blood of Jesus Christ?

    Response: This is too easy. There has never been a time where the Church ever said the Eucharist was not the Body and Blood of Jesus Christ.

2) The belief in the Real Presence was not localized to one area of the Roman Empire. What modern day countries were catechized by the Apostles through the Early Church Fathers?
    Response: Here are a few (neglecting Sts. Peter and Paul—Israel (St. Jerome), India (St Thomas), Spain (St James the Greater), Algeria, (St Augustine), Turkey (St Ignatius of Antioch), France (St Irenaus), Egypt (St Clement of Alexandria) Syria (St John of Damascus), Crete (St Barnabas), Lebanon (St Maron)

Chapter 7: Questions for Discussion

1) This chapter discussed the *sacramentum tantum* of Baptism and of the Eucharist. What would be the various *sacramentum tantum* of the sacrament of Marriage, the sacrament of Confirmation (or Chrismation), the sacrament of Reconciliation, the sacrament of Holy Orders, and the sacrament of Anointing of the Sick?

   Response: The sacramentum tantum of marriage would be the vows and marital act (under normal conditions, a marriage must be consummated). For Confirmation it is chrism, the laying on of hands, and the invocation of the Holy Spirit. For Reconciliation it is heartfelt contrition, the confession of sins, followed by the satisfaction (completion of penance), and the words of absolution. For Holy Orders, it is the laying on of hands and the consecratory preface. For the Anointing of the sick, it is the anointing with oil and the priestly prayers.

2) The various beliefs found in Christianity concerning the Eucharist belie the one aspect lacking in all non-Catholic/non-Orthodox Christian churches. What is that aspect?

   Response: Jesus established a "sacerdotal" priesthood, that is, a priesthood which is to offer sacrifice, when he commanded the Apostles (and thereby, their successors) to "Do this." At each Mass, the priest operates "*in Persona*

Christi." The offering of Jesus, by Jesus Himself as Victim and High Priest, acting through the priest, to the Father for the atonement of sin is for all time and is therefore, outside of time. The very sacrifice of the Mass <u>IS</u> the very sacrifice at Golgotha. While Christ's atonement is sufficient (he doesn't need us), at Mass, we are able to join our sufferings with Christ in this offering.

Chapter 8: Questions for Discussion

1) Maybe you can help me out here. The Eucharistic miracle at Lanciano has been around for 1300 years (impossible) and has been studied scientifically as to what the nature of the muscle and the blood are. The artifact of the muscle is somehow attached to the rim of bread (impossible). How can anyone deny this miracle? Certainly, no one can duplicate it.

   If you discover a way to attach muscle to bread and not have it decay, be sure to contact me and the world.

2) There is a Vatican-approved exhibit that presents to the faithful over 200 Eucharistic miracles. True, many have no physical evidence left behind, but many do? Is it likely that all are liars?

   One would have to be pretty skeptical to believe all individuals involved in past Eucharistic miracles are liars or were fooled. Of course, the miracles with remaining evidence give support for those instances which have no evidence left behind.

Chapter 9: Questions for Discussion

1) What do you remember of your first Holy Communion?

   This is for you to recall. Napoleon Bonaparte said it was the happiest day of his life.

2) What do you remember of your last Holy Communion?

   Hopefully, if you can remember what you had for breakfast, you might also remember and will be able to reflect on your preparation, reception, and thoughts that you had.

Chapter 10: Questions for Discussion

1) Many people are skeptical of healing miracles. True, there are cases in which psychological issues may result in thinking one has had a miraculous healing; however, some are so well documented, as in the examples of Chapter 10. How can one convince the eternal skeptic?

   We can only present evidence. In the end the Holy Spirit will provide the graces which the individual will accept or not.

2) I have been told many times by physicians that the study of the body, and incidents in the care of their patients have convinced them that there must be a supreme being far greater than us. Have you ever asked your physician if they have ever witnessed such an apparently incredible event?

Go ahead and ask. You may be surprised at their answers.

Chapter 11: Questions for Discussion

1) How has the Eucharist affected your life?

The answer to that is for you to share.

Appendix B

List of Figures

10.3	A young, healthy Brother Leo Schwager
10.4	Brother Leo Schwager in 1996
10.5	A young, healthy Jeanne Fretel
10.6	Jeanne Fretel years after her miraculous recovery

Appendix C

Suggested Reading

Books:

Akin, Jimmy. *The Fathers Know Best*. El Cajon, CA: Catholic Answers, Inc., 2010.

Aquilina, Mike. *The Mass of the Early Christians*. Huntington, IN: Our Sunday Visitor, 2001.

Benedict XVI. *Jesus of Nazareth*. Vol. 1. New York: Doubleday, 2007.

Cruz, Joan. *Eucharistic Miracles*. Rockford, IL: Tan Books and Publishers, 1987.

Glynn, Paul. *The Healing Fire of Christ*. San Francisco: Ignatius Press, 2003.

Hahn, Scott. *The Lamb's Supper*. New York: Doubleday, 1999.

Jurgens, William. *The Faith of the Early Fathers*. Vol. 1–3. Collegeville, MN: Liturgical Press, 1970.

O'Connor, James, Rev. *The Hidden Manna*, 2nd ed. San Francisco: Ignatius Press, 2005.

Pitre, Brant. *Jesus and the Jewish Roots of the Eucharist*. New York: Random House, 2011.

Wolf, Fred A. *Taking the Quantum Leap*. New York: Harper and Row, 1989.

Woods, Thomas, Jr. *How the Catholic Church Built Western Civilization*. Washington, DC: Regnery Publishing, 2005.

Encyclicals:

Leo XIII. *Mirae Caritatis*. 1902.
Pius XII. *Christus Dominus*. 1953.
Paul VI. *Mysterium Fidei*. 1995.
John Paul II. *Fides et Ratio*. 1998.
John Paul II. *Ecclesia Eucharista*. 2003.

Websites:

Reservation of the Blessed Sacrament.
http://www.newadvent.org/cathen/12784b.htm.
Adoremus Bulletin.
http://www.adoremus.org/0707SupersubstantialBread.html

Index

A

Abraham, 65, 82

Acts of the apostles, 85, 94, 162

Adam, 26-8, 65

agape (love) feasts, 87, 98-9

Alan of Lille, 135

Albigensians, 134, 137

Alexander II (pope), 131

Alexander III (pope), 135

Ambrose, Saint, 108, 113, 130

anamnesis, 70, 93-4

Anglican Church, 142, 145

Antonius Pius (Emperor), 163

Aphrahat, 111

apostles, 3, 5, 22-4, 43-4, 46-9, 54-
5, 59, 68-9, 71, 73, 75, 77,
79, 81, 83-5, 89, 92, 94-5,
99, 101-3, 118, 121, 124,
127, 131-2, 134, 139, 150,
162, 165, 168

Apostolic Fathers, 3, 75, 99, 101

See also Early Church Fathers

Arians, 117

Aristotle, 136

ark of the covenant, 29, 35

Ascension, 24, 53, 57, 114

Attila the Hun, 82-3

Augustine, Saint, 18, 25, 113-14,
118, 123-6, 129-30, 171,
174, 192

B

Baptism of Desire, 59

Beatitudes, 27

beauty, 11-2, 14, 177

Benedict XVI (pope), 60, 62

Berengarius of Tours, 129-32

Bergoglio, Bishop Jorge, 155

Bible, 5, 21, 99, 101-03, 136, 168

See also New Testament; Old
Testament

big bang theory, 7, 157

Blessed Virgin Mary, 179

bread

Bread of the Presence, 35-6,
40, 174

bread-of-life discourse, 48,
50-1, 60

breaking of, 6, 77, 86, 88, 95-
9, 104, 162-63

daily, 59

and wine, 1, 6, 21, 28, 30-1,
36, 40, 44, 66, 69, 72,
78, 86, 90-91, 112, 115-
16, 126, 128, 130-32,
138-39, 141, 143-44,
145, 150-51, 153, 164-

213